English Simplified

THIRTEENTH EDITION

Blanche Ellsworth

Late, San Francisco State University

John A. Higgins

York College, City University of New York (Retired)

PEARSON

Boston   Columbus   Indianapolis   New York   San Francisco   Upper Saddle River
Amsterdam   Cape Town   Dubai   London   Madrid   Milan   Munich   Paris   Montréal   Toronto
Delhi   Mexico City   São Paulo   Sydney   Hong Kong   Seoul   Singapore   Taipei   Tokyo

PREFACE

What's New in the Thirteenth Edition?

- Refinements and additions to coverage of clarity in writing, both in Part 4 and throughout the text.
- New real-life examples of unclear prose that underscore the importance of clarity.
- Extensive revisions to Part 5 that provide a fresh and current perspective on electronic research.
- New examples of paragraph, essay, and research paper development in Part 5.
- A guide to the 2009 edition of the MLA guidelines for research papers.
- A guide to the 2010 edition of the APA's style rules.

The thirteenth edition of *English Simplified* takes a giant step into the electronic age. Nearly every section of the book now contains a prompt guiding students to related content in *MyWritingLab*. Wherever the "open door" icon appears, instructions at the end of the section provide a pathway to online learning tools and interactive practice.

In content, *English Simplified*, 13th edition, continues and refines the revisions of the twelfth edition, particularly the emphasis on clarity in writing. "Clarity is a writer's first obligation," advises the introduction to the "Clarity and Smoothness" section. "If you are not clear, you are not communicating." How to make one's writing clearer is emphasized not just in this section but throughout the book: in the sections on clear pronoun reference, unclear modifiers, illogical or confused sentence construction, omitted needed words, confusing punctuation, cluttered sentences, buried subjects, possessives with understood nouns, overuse of negatives, exaggerated or needless modifiers (*awesome, totally, iconic*...), and unclear paragraph structure.

Learning from examples—of both bad writing and good—is the key to students' comprehending the principles of good writing. *English Simplified* is filled with such examples, scores of them new or updated.

Published works, unfortunately, have become an increasing source for examples of garbled writing—some of them quite chuckleworthy, as in the tourist brochure I picked up that declared, "Nearing collapse, having been idle for almost forty years, Mr. and Mrs. X bought the mill in 1992 and began restoration." *English Simplified* makes copious use of such gaffes to underscore the need for clarity.

The most extensively redone section in *English Simplified* is part 5, "Paragraphs and Papers." Emily Thomas, of Emerson College, Boston, has been enlisted to provide a fresh perspective on the fast-changing field of electronic research and its related matters. Part 5 incorporates both her text revisions and her new examples of paragraph, essay, and research-paper development. It also includes the most recent revisions of research-paper bibliographic style, as shown in the *MLA Handbook for Writers of Research Papers*, seventh edition (2009), and in the American Psychological Association's *Concise Rules of APA Style* (2010).

Acknowledgments

The editors and I believe you will find *English Simplified,* 13th edition, a valuable compact guide to clear, correct, and effective writing. For additional practice, an *Exercise Book for English Simplified,* 13th edition (0-205-07482-0; *Answer Key,* 0-205-11048-7), is also available.

Many of the improvements mentioned come from reviewers' suggestions. I would like to thank Marie Eckstrom, Rio Hondo College; Amy Hundley, Merced College; Bonnie Devet, College of Charleston; Lindsey Pilgreen, University of La Verne; Charles F. Warren, Salem State University; Jack Lawson, California State University, Fresno; Pamela Howell, Midland College; and Helen Smith, Kentucky State University.

My thanks go also to my ever-patient wife, Elizabeth, for reading the manuscript and advising sensible changes; to my sons Bob and Brendan for keeping me abreast of what is popular with younger adults; and to the Pearson editorial staff for their excellent support and guidance in preparing this edition.

JOHN A. HIGGINS

Senior Acquisitions Editor: Matthew Wright
Assistant Editor: Amanda Dykstra
Marketing Manager: Kurt Massey
Executive Digital Producer: Stefanie A. Snajder

Senior Supplements Editor: Donna Campion
Production Manager: Savoula Amanatidis
Project Coordination, Text Design, and Electronic
  Page Makeup: Integra Software Services, Inc.

Cover Designer/Manager: John Callahan
Senior Manufacturing Buyer: Dennis J. Para
Printer & Binder: Courier Corporation–Westford
Cover Printer: Courier Corporation–Westford

Library of Congress Cataloging-in-Publication Data
Ellsworth, Blanche, 1902–1997.
  English simplified / Blanche Ellsworth, John A. Higgins.—13th ed.
    p. cm.
  Includes index.
  ISBN-13: 978-0-205-11046-9
  ISBN-10: 0-205-11046-0
  1. English language—Grammar—Handbooks, manuals, etc.   2. English language—Punctuation—Handbooks, manuals, etc.   3. English language—Textbooks for foreign speakers.   I. Higgins, John A.   II. Title.

PE1112.E43 2012
425—dc23   2011022592

10 9 8 7 6 5 4 3 2 1—CRW—15 14 13 12

ISBN-10:   0-205-11046-0
ISBN-13: 978-0-205-11046-9

In the newspaper an FBI agent had a shootout with a smuggler, he died from his wounds.

Buzzing around the ceiling, Joyce found the fly was disturbing her concentration and couldn't tolerate it.

As a household pet, I think a Doberman is a poor choice around children, because they attack and bite when annoyed.

Can you tell what is wrong with each of these sentences? Well-intentioned adults too often write sentences like these, thinking them clear and correct. Without an understanding of the basic grammar of the English sentence, we can easily fall into such pitfalls of language. Part 1 of *English Simplified* explains essential grammar concisely, in the most common terms, to help you create sentences that are not only correct but clear and effective.

101–103. The Sentence and Its Parts

101. The Two Parts of a Sentence. The **sentence** is our basic unit of spoken or written thought:

> The mayor dedicated a new bridge yesterday.
> How long did she speak?
> What an impressive structure it is!

(A written sentence always begins with a capital letter and ends with a period [.], question mark [?], or exclamation point [!].)

A sentence expresses a *complete* thought. To do so, it must have two parts: **subject** and **verb.**

101A. The Subject. The **subject** names the topic of the sentence. It tells what the sentence is talking about. The subject may be one or more persons, things, places, or ideas—such as *girl, Sally Sanders, mayor, computer, mountains, Paris, despair, you, she, it.*

> *Note:* *Girl* and the other words just above are called *nouns*-- except *you, she,* and it, which are *pronouns.* Section 104, page 3, tells more about these kinds of words.

Subject (in **bold** type)

> A **crowd** gathered. [Sentence is talking about a *crowd.*]
> A noisy, happy **crowd** gathered around the victors yesterday. [still talking about a *crowd*]
> Persuasive **commercials** on television increased sales of our product. [talking about *commercials*]
> My father's old **diploma** from State College still hangs on our living-room wall. [talking about a *diploma.*]
> **You** may see the personnel director now. [talking about *you*]

The subject word and any surrounding words that relate to it make up together the **complete subject:**

Subject (in **bold**) *Complete subject* (in box)

> A noisy, happy **crowd** gathered around the victors yesterday.
> Persuasive **commercials** on television increased sales of our product.
> My father's old **diploma** from State College still hangs on our living-room wall.
> **You** may see the personnel director now.

> *Note:* Only the most common kind of sentence, the kind that *tells* something, is shown here. In section 103A you will meet sentences that *ask, command,* and *exclaim.* For simplicity, most sentence discussions in this book will deal with sentences that *tell* something (declarative sentences).

101B. The Verb. The **verb** asserts something about the subject; mostly, it tells what the subject does (or did, or will do), such as *cheer, rise, walk, dedicate, recognize, go, gather:*

Verb

> A crowd **gathered**. [Sentence is telling what the crowd *did.*]
> A noisy, happy crowd **gathered** around the victors yesterday. [still telling what the crowd *did*]
> Persuasive commercials on television **increased** sales of our product. [telling what the commercials *did*]
> My father's old diploma from State College still **hangs** on our living-room wall. [telling what the diploma *does*]
> You **may see** the personnel director now. [telling what you *may do*]

Another name for the verb is the **predicate.** The verb and any surrounding words that relate to it make up together the **complete predicate:**

Verb (predicate) (in **bold**) *Complete predicate* (in box)

> A noisy, happy crowd **gathered** around the victors yesterday.
> Persuasive commercials on television **increased** sales of our product.
> My father's old diploma from State College still **hangs** on our living-room wall.
> You **may see** the personnel director now.

> *Note:* **Verbs of being.** A few verbs assert *being* instead of doing: *is, am, are, was, been, seem.* . . .
>
> > Abby's new car **is** a hybrid. [Here the car is not doing anything; rather it is *being* something.]
>
> Such verbs, called **linking verbs,** are explained in section 114C (page 7).

Completers of the verb. Some verbs need other words (in the complete predicate) to complete their meaning:

> Several freshmen *staged* . . . [Staged what? Meaning is not complete.]
> Several freshmen *staged* a **protest.** [Staged what? *Protest* (completer).]

Our favorite movie star *is* . . . [Is who? Meaning is not complete.]

Our favorite movie star *is* **Matt Damon.** [Is who? *Matt Damon* (completer).]

Section 112, page 5, explains subjects and verb completers; section 105, page 3, and sections 113–118, pages 6–13, explain verbs.

Note: Many sentence parts may be **compound;** that is, they may have two or more elements joined by *and, or,* or *but*:

Compound subject: Both **men** and **women** reside at this college.

Compound verb: This college **enrolls** and **graduates** students from diverse backgrounds.

Compound complete predicate: Students at this college **study hard for their degrees** but also **enjoy a lively social life.**

---

102. The Sentence Pattern.
Subject, verb, and any verb completers usually appear in a fixed order, or pattern: **S V (C) (C).** This means that the subject [**S**] comes first, then the verb [**V**], then—perhaps—one or two verb completers [**C**]:

       S   V

The nation's *leaders assembled* hurriedly.

     S   V

Retail *prices* of consumer goods often *rise* before the holidays.

    S   V   C

Students in English 101 *write* a ten-page *paper.*

    S   V   C   C

Noises from the street *gave her* a *headache.*

     S   V

My *brother has* just *arrived* from Afghanistan.

This usual order is altered in

               S   V   C

Most questions: *What did they see?* [→ *They did see what?*]

              S V

Many exclamations: Such a *fool I was!* [→ *I was* such

  C

a *fool!*]

Sentences such as these:

            S   V

Never *had we seen* such *chaos.* [→ *We had* never *seen*

  C

such *chaos.*]

              S V

There *were* no *seats* anywhere. [→ No *seats were* anywhere.]

103. Ways of Classifying Sentences

103A. By Purpose

Declarative (a statement): The plane is leaving on time.

Interrogative (a question): Is the plane leaving on time?

Imperative (a command or request): Board the plane now. Be alert. [*You* is understood to be the subject.]

Exclamatory (an expression of emotion, often beginning with *how* or *what*): What a clear night for flying! How smooth this flight is!

103B. By Structure.
A **clause** is one unit of *complete subject + complete predicate.* Each sentence you have studied so far has just one clause:

Several *freshmen staged* a protest.

Noisy, happy *crowds gathered* around the victors yesterday.

Such a one-clause sentence is called a **simple sentence.**

A sentence joining two or more simple-sentence clauses is called a **compound sentence.** Below, each clause is boxed:

Several *freshmen staged* a protest, but most *students ignored it.*

Some *freshmen distributed* leaflets, *others picketed* the office, and *many planned* a rally.

A sentence with one or more clauses dependent on a main clause is called a **complex sentence:**

Dependent clause

(not a complete thought by itself— must be joined to main clause)

Main (independent) clause

Several *freshmen staged* a protest when the *dean suspended* Max.

Others distributed leaflets that the *protesters had written.*

Note: A sentence combining a compound and a complex sentence is called a **compound-complex sentence:**

Several *freshmen staged* a protest, and *others distributed* leaflets that the *protesters had written.*

For a fuller explanation of clauses, see section 125, page 20.

For resources to help you master this section's topics, log in to www.mywritinglab.com and select Subjects and Verbs from the list of subtopics.

104–110. The Parts of Speech: A Survey

Traditional English grammar divides all words into eight **parts of speech** according to how each word functions in its sentence:

Nouns and **pronouns** name things.

Verbs assert (express doing or being).

Adjectives and **adverbs** modify (describe or limit).
Conjunctions and **prepositions** connect.
Interjections exclaim.

To write effectively, you need to understand these parts of speech and how they relate to one another.

104. Nouns and Pronouns: Words That Name

104A. Nouns. A noun is a word that names a person, place, or thing (including a quality or idea):

> **Person:** author, cousin, Rachel Perez, vice president
> **Place:** island, Hawaii, firehouse, closet, Elm Street
> **Thing:** wrench, oatmeal, building, zebra, Sphinx
> **Quality or idea:** love, height, liberty, motion, cleverness

See 111–112, page 5, for details about nouns.

104B. Pronouns. A pronoun takes the place of (stands for) a noun. That noun is called the **antecedent** of the pronoun. Below, an arrow points from the pronoun to its antecedent:

> *Rosa* brought a friend with **her** to the rally.

> When the *trees* turn color, **they** bring out hordes of leaf-peepers.

Pronouns include such words as *I, me, myself, we, you, he, his, she, it, them, who, this, everyone, all.*

See 121–123, pages 15–19, for details about pronouns.

105. Verbs: Words That Express Doing or Being.

A verb asserts something about the subject of a sentence. An **action verb** tells what the subject *does, did,* or *will do.* A **linking verb** tells that the subject *is, was,* or *will be* something.

> **Action:** Antonia *plays* her guitar at the café Friday nights. [tells what the subject, *Antonia,* does]
> **Linking:** Antonia *is* a skilled guitarist. [tells that the subject is something]

Some verbs contain two or more words: a **main verb** preceded by one or more **auxiliary** (helping) **verbs:**

> *Auxiliary verb(s)* (in *italics*) Main verb (in **bold**)
> Antonia *has* **played** there for a year.
> She *will* soon *be* **leaving** for graduate school.

> *Note:* A verb of more than one word is sometimes referred to as a **verb phrase.**

See 113–118, pages 6–13, for details about verbs.

> *Note:* Besides asserting (in a declarative or exclamatory sentence), a verb can also *ask* (in an interrogative sentence) or *command* or *request* (in an imperative sentence).

106. Adjectives and Adverbs: Words That Modify.

To *modify* means "to change." A modifying word changes or clarifies our concept of another word.

106A. Adjectives. An adjective modifies a noun (or occasionally a pronoun). It describes that noun or limits its meaning.

Descriptive adjectives tell *what kind of:*

> *bumpy* road [what kind of road?]
> *energetic* teenagers [what kind of teenagers?]
> *incredible* courage [what kind of courage?]
> *long, boring* speech [what kind of speech?]

Limiting adjectives (sometimes called **determiners**) tell *which one(s), how many,* or *how much.* There are several kinds of limiting adjectives:

> **Possessive:** *my* auto, *her* grades, *their* policy [tells which auto, grades, policy]
> **Demonstrative:** *this* auto, *those* grades, *that* policy
> **Indefinite:** *any* auto, *either* grade, *many* policies
> **Interrogative:** *which* auto? *whose* grades? *what* policy?
> **Numerical:** *one* auto, *two* grades, *third* policy
> **Articles:** *an* auto, *the* grades, *a* policy

As these examples show, an adjective usually appears directly before the noun it modifies. A descriptive adjective can appear also after a linking verb (as a verb completer describing the subject):

> **s   v   c**
> This notice is *unclear.* [*Unclear* describes the subject, *notice.*]
> The information seemed *reliable.*

106B. Adverbs. An adverb usually modifies a verb. It describes *how, when, where,* or *to what degree* the action of a verb is done. There are several kinds of adverbs:

> **Manner:** Kayla practices *intensely.* [practices how?]
> **Time:** Kayla practiced *yesterday.* [practiced when?]
> **Place:** Kayla practices *everywhere.* [practices where?]
> **Degree:** Kayla practices *excessively.* [practices to what extent or degree?]

> *Note:* An adverb phrase or clause can also describe *why:* Kayla practices *to make the team.* (Sections 124–125, page 19, explain phrases and clauses.)

Some adverbs can modify an adjective or another adverb. Such adverbs are called **adverbs of degree** (or **intensifiers** or **qualifiers**):

> Kayla practices *quite* vigorously. [vigorously to what degree? how vigorously?]
> Kayla enjoys *very* vigorous workouts. [how vigorous?]

> *Note:* Special kinds of adverbs include **conjunctive adverbs** (see 210B, page 36), **sentence adverbs** (see 201B, page 31), and **relative adverbs** (see 125B, page 20).

107. Conjunctions and Prepositions: Words That Connect

107A. Conjunctions. A conjunction joins other words or word groups. There are two main kinds of conjunctions:

A coordinating conjunction (*and, but, or, nor, for, yet, so*) joins words or word groups of the same kind and same importance:

> **Words:** Pam *and* George
> **Word groups (phrases):** in the kitchen *and* on the back porch
> **Word groups (clauses):** They cooked in the kitchen, *but* they ate on the back porch.

> *Note: And, but, or,* or *nor* may be used with other words to form a **correlative conjunction:** *not only . . . but also; (n)either . . . (n)or; both . . . and:*
>
> > *Both* Pam *and* George like baked eggplant.
> > *Neither* Pam *nor* George likes fried food.

See 402C, page 52, on using *so*. See 124–125, pages 19–21, for definitions of *phrase* and *clause*.

A subordinating conjunction (*if, because, although, when, unless,* and others) joins a dependent (subordinate) clause to an independent (main) clause. The subordinating conjunction begins the dependent clause: *if her cell phone is on; because her cell phone was off.*

> We can inform her *if her cell phone is on.*
> *If her cell phone is on,* we can inform her.
> She never found out *because her cell phone was off.*
> *Because her cell phone was off,* she never found out.
> *When the rope broke,* I fell. I fell *when the rope broke.*

> *Caution:* Writing a dependent clause alone, as if it were a complete sentence, is a serious error, called a *fragment:*
>
> > *Fragment*
> > **Wrong:** Your absence will be excused. *If you submit a doctor's note.*
> > **Right:** Your absence will be excused *if you submit a doctor's note.*

Section 129A, page 26, explains how to avoid fragments.

Other common subordinating conjunctions are

after	provided	whenever
as (if)	since	where
as soon as	so that	whereas
as though	than	wherever
before	(al)though	whether
in order that	until	while

See 125A, B, page 20; 128D, page 24; and 129, page 26, for more on dependent (subordinate) clauses.

> *Note:* Other kinds of words that join clauses are **relative pronouns** (*who, which* . . .—see 125B, page 20) and **conjunctive adverbs** (*therefore, however* . . .—see 210B, page 36).

107B. Prepositions. A preposition is a connecting word (such as *in, on, of, for,* or *into*) showing how the noun that follows it is related to another part of the sentence:

> *Preposition*   *Noun*
> Snow fell **on** the old *house.*
> The family stayed **in** the old *house.*
> Wind whistled **through** the old *house.*
> Weeds grew **around** the old *house.*

Each preposition above shows a different relation between the noun *house* and the action of the sentence. Other common prepositions are

about	beside	instead of	toward
above	besides	like	under
against	between	near	underneath
among	by	next to	until
as	despite	off	up
as well as	down	onto	upon
at	during	out (of)	with
because of	except	outside	within
before	from	past	without
behind	in addition to	since	
below	in front of	throughout	
beneath	inside	to	

The whole word group, from the preposition to the following noun, is called a **prepositional phrase** (boxed in examples below). The noun (or pronoun) is called the **object of the preposition:**

> *Preposition* (in **bold**)   *Object of prep.* (in *italics*)
> The diplomats met **at** the *White House*.
> Freshmen **with** financial *problems* should go **to** *her*.

For more on objects of prepositions, see 112C, page 6.

> *Note:* The word *to* followed by a verb (we tried *to talk* to her) is not a prepositional phrase; it is called an **infinitive.** You will learn about infinitives in section 117A, page 12.

Prepositions of Time, Place, and Travel |ESL|

	Time	Place	Means of Travel
at	*a specific moment:*	*a particular spot:*	
	at 9:45	at home; at work	
	at noon	at the store	
		at Fifth and Main	
		at the end	
on	*a day or date:*	*the top or surface of:*	on a bicycle
	on Monday	on Main Street	on a bus
	on May 5	on the roof	on a ship
		on Long Island	on a plane
		on the ocean	on a train
in	*a period of time:*	*(within) an area:*	in a car
	in a week	in jail; in bed	in a carriage
	in 2012	in her office	in a canoe
		in Iowa	

108. Interjections: Words That Exclaim. Unlike the other kinds of words, an interjection has no grammatical connection with the rest of the sentence:

> ***Mild interjection*** (punctuated with comma): *Oh,* I don't care. *Well,* Dr. Lopez might know.
> ***Strong interjection*** (punctuated with exclamation point): *Rats!* He's cheated us. *Wow!* It's snowing.

109. A Word as Different Parts of Speech. We label each word by what it does in a particular sentence: if it names something, it is a noun; if it describes a noun, it is an adjective, and so forth:

> ***Noun:*** The *display* was colorful.
> ***Verb:*** *Display* your passport.
>
> ***Noun:*** The *light* flickered out.
> ***Verb:*** They *light* a fire every evening.
> ***Adjective:*** We could feel a *light* breeze.

Note: A word's position in a sentence or a word's ending is often (though not always) a clue to its part of speech. For example:

- A word following a limiting adjective (*my, this . . .*) is likely to be a noun: *my* **brother,** *this* **test** (another adjective may come between them: *this* impossible **test**).
- A word following an auxiliary verb is likely to be a verb: *has* **grown,** *might have been* **injured** (an adverb may come between: *might have been* severely **injured**).
- A word with an *-ly* ending is likely to be an adverb: slow*ly,* awkward*ly,* inexorab*ly.*
- A word ending in *-tion, -ity, -ness, -ment, -hood,* or *-cy* is usually a noun: condi*tion,* equal*ity,* happi*ness,* argu*ment,* state*hood,* poli*cy.*
- A word ending in *-ify* or *-ize* is probably a verb: identi*fy,* harmon*ize.*
- A word ending in *-al, -ous, -ful,* or *-less* is probably an adjective: chor*al,* joy*ous,* hope*ful,* hope*less.*

---

110. A Word Group as a Part of Speech. A group of words (a phrase or clause) can act as a single word:

Noun:	Phrase or clause acting as noun:
His **answer** surprised everyone.	**His accepting the blame** surprised everyone. **What he told us** surprised everyone.
Adjective (describing *cathedral*): We visited an **ancient** cathedral.	Phrase or clause acting as adjective: We visited a cathedral **built in 1102.** We visited a cathedral **that the Normans built.**
Adverb (modifying *ran*): She ran **desperately.**	Phrase or clause acting as adverb: She ran **in desperation.** She ran **as if tigers were chasing her.**

You have already met clauses in section 103B and prepositional phrases in 107B; you will learn more about phrases and clauses in 124 and 125, pages 19–21.

For resources to help you master this section's topics, log in to www.mywritinglab.com and select The Parts of Speech, Phrases and Clauses from the list of subtopics.

111–112. Using Nouns

Recall that nouns name persons, places, or things.

111. The Kinds of Nouns. Nouns are classified in several ways:

111A. Singular or Plural. A **singular** noun names one person, place, or thing: *actor, island, snowshoe, mouse, Elmer.* A **plural** noun names two or more persons, places, or things: *actors, islands, snowshoes, mice.* Most singular nouns become plural by the addition of *-s.* See 312, page 48, for rules on forming plurals.

111B. Common or Proper. A **common** noun names one or more members of a class of things: *actor, actors, island, mouse, auditorium.* A **proper** noun names a specific person, place, or thing: *Meryl Streep, Catalina Island, Mickey Mouse, Carnegie Hall.*

111C. Concrete or Abstract. A **concrete** noun names an object that can be perceived by the senses: *actor, Meryl Streep, mice, opera, odor, wind.* An **abstract** noun names a quality or idea: *liberty, sadness, ambition, love, tragedy, height.*

111D. Collective. A **collective** noun names a group of things: *jury, team, flock, committee, army.*

111E. Count or Noncount. See 120B, page 15.

112. The Uses of Nouns. Recall the basic sentence pattern you learned in section 102: **S V (C) (C).** That is, each sentence has a *subject,* a *verb,* and perhaps one or two *verb completers.* Nouns serve as subjects and completers and do several other jobs as well.

112A. The Subject of a Sentence. Recall that the **subject** names the person or thing that the sentence is talking about. The subject is the noun (or pronoun) that tells *who* or *what* is doing or being something:

> *Subject*   *Verb*
> **Scientists** *studied* the newly found virus. [Who studied?]
> This **virus** *was infecting* forest deer. [What was infecting?]
> Last month **Drs. Katz** and **Jackson** *had isolated* the virus. [Who had isolated? (compound subject)]
> Their brilliant **work** *made* them famous around the world. [What made?]

112B. A Verb Completer. This is a word (in the complete predicate) that completes the meaning of the verb. (Not all verbs have completers.) There are four kinds of verb completers:

direct object	indirect object
subject complement	object complement

A **direct object** is a noun (or pronoun) needed to complete the meaning of some action verbs. It answers *whom* or *what* after the verb; that is, it tells who or what is receiving the verb's action:

Subject   Verb   Direct object

Scientists studied the newly found **virus.** [studied what?]

The *Medical Society commended* **Drs. Katz** and **Jackson.** [commended whom?]

Around the world, *environmentalists praised* their brilliant **work.** [praised what?]

For more on direct objects, see 114A.

An **indirect object** is a noun (or pronoun) that may follow certain action verbs. It tells *to* (or *for*) *whom* or *what* the action of the verb is done. It ordinarily precedes the direct object:

Subject   Verb   Indirect obj.   Direct obj.

Love-smitten *Homer sent* **Myrtle** twelve *roses.* [sent to whom?]

The *builders gave* the **house** a slate *roof.* [gave to what?]

Party *workers did* the **mayor** a *favor.* [did for whom?]

Our local theater *group gave* the **United Fund** a benefit *performance.* [gave for what?]

A **subject complement** is a noun (or pronoun) that follows a linking verb. It renames or explains the subject:

Subject   Verb   Subject comp.

Amelia Pagan is our class **president**. [*Amelia Pagan = president. President* is another name or title for *Amelia Pagan.*]

A *neophyte is* a **beginner**. [*Neophyte = beginner. Beginner* explains what *neophyte* is.]

> *Note:* A subject complement can also be an adjective: *Amelia Pagan is* extremely **competent.**

For more on linking verbs and subject complements, see 114C.

An **object complement** is a noun that may follow a direct object to rename or explain it:

Subject   Verb   Dir. obj.   Object comp.

The *class elected Amelia Pagan* **president**. [*Amelia Pagan = president. President* is another name or title for *Amelia Pagan.*]

Opponents consider her *election* a **mistake**. [*Election = mistake.*]

The object complement occurs most commonly with such verbs as *call, name, designate, elect, consider, appoint, think.*

> *Note:* An object complement can also be an adjective: Opponents *called* her *election* **unfortunate.**

112C. An Object of a Preposition is a noun (or pronoun) that ends a prepositional phrase and answers the question *whom* or *what* after the preposition:

Ms. Roy met with her **publisher**. [with whom?]

Stores in **town** struggle against new **malls**. [in what? against what?]

See 107 B, page 4, for more on prepositions.

112D. An Appositive is a second noun that renames or further identifies a nearby first noun:

First noun   Appositive

Amelia Pagan, the new **president,** has grand plans for our class. [*President* is another name or title for *Amelia Pagan.* It is an appositive (or *in apposition*) to *Amelia Pagan.*]

First noun   Appositive

We bought a new *car,* a **Ford**.

The *hotel* they booked, the **Commodore,** proved too expensive.

They were forced to stay at the *Purple Palace,* the one **motel** they were trying to avoid.

For punctuation of appositives, see 201F, page 32.

112E. Direct Address. A noun (or pronoun) in **direct address** names the person being spoken to:

Noun: **Amelia,** the dean wants to see you.

Pronoun: Come over here, **you!**

For resources to help you master this section's topics, log in to www.mywritinglab.com and select Nouns from the list of subtopics.

113–118. Using Verbs

The verb is the core of every sentence. Without a verb, a group of words is only a sentence fragment, not a complete sentence. Recall that a verb asserts something about its subject—that is, it tells what the subject *does* (*did, will do*) or that the subject *is* (*was, will be*) something:

My car **rattles.** [What does the car do?]

The Senate **voted** the bill into law. [What did the Senate do?]

The local volcanoes **were** frequently **spewing** lava. [What were the volcanoes doing?]

Fred **is** Clarissa's new boyfriend. [Fred is being the boyfriend.]

What **did** they **argue** about? [What did they do? An interrogative sentence asks rather than tells.]

Find me a seat in the front row, please. [In an imperative sentence, the subject is understood to be *you:* (You) **find** me a seat.]

For a review of the kinds of verbs, see 105, page 3.

113. Identifying the Verb.
There is a simple way to identify the verb in a sentence. The verb is the word that will usually change its form if you change the time of the sentence:

This week the team *practices* daily.

Last week they *practiced* daily.

Next week they *will practice* daily.

For the last five weeks they *have practiced* daily.

114. The Kinds of Verbs.
A verb is classified according to the kind of completer (if any) that follows it. In addition, there is a special kind of verb called an **auxiliary** (or helping) verb that may accompany a main verb.

114A. A Transitive Verb is an action verb that needs a direct object to complete its meaning. That is, it expresses an action that passes across (transits) from a doer (do-er, the subject—the person or thing that does the action) to a receiver (the direct object—the person or thing that is on the receiving end of the action):

Subject (doer)   Verb   Direct object (receiver)

The *broker telephoned* his **clients**. [Broker telephoned whom? *Clients* is the direct object.]
Red *lights stop* **traffic**. [Lights stop what?]
Homer sent Myrtle twelve **roses**. [Homer sent what?]

114B. An Intransitive Verb is one that does not need a direct object to complete its meaning. It expresses an action that does not have a receiver:

The meeting *adjourned.*
Yesterday the value of our stocks *rose.*
The chairperson *stayed* after the meeting. [*After the meeting* is a prepositional phrase, telling when. It is not a direct object.]
Pollutants *act* insidiously. [*Insidiously* is an adverb, telling how. It is not a direct object.]

> **Note:** Many verbs can be transitive in some uses (Mary *stopped* the *fight*) and intransitive in others (Mary suddenly *stopped*). Dictionaries label each meaning of a verb as *v.t.* (verb, transitive) or *v.i.* (verb, intransitive).

114C. A Linking Verb expresses no action at all; it merely links what comes before the verb (the subject) and what comes after it (the subject complement). It says that these two are the same (Jared *is* my brother) or that the one describes the other (Jared *is* brilliant):

Hoosick Falls *is* their new home. [*Hoosick Falls = home.*]
Her cousin *became* a minister. [*Cousin = minister.*]
Their last performance *was* quite impressive. [*Impressive* describes *performance.*]

The chief linking verb is *be.* Its parts are

am   is   are   was   were   being   been

Other linking verbs are those roughly like *be* in meaning—

seem   appear   remain   prove   become   grow   turn

—and the verbs of the five senses:

look   sound   feel   smell   taste

Her fried concoction *was* (*appeared, looked, smelled, tasted, became, turned*) rancid.

Some verbs may be linking verbs in one sense and action verbs in another:

Linking	*Action*
He *looked* tired.	He *looked* out the window.
Ahmed *grew* pensive.	Ahmed *grew* tomatoes.

114D. An Auxiliary (Helping) Verb. A verb may contain more than one word, as in *has fallen, is walking, did try,* or *could have helped.* The last word in such a verb is the **main verb.** Any preceding words in the verb are called **auxiliary verbs,** or simply **auxiliaries.** Each auxiliary helps express the precise meaning of the main verb.

Only a few verbs can be auxiliaries:

- *Have (has, had).* After these, the main verb uses its *-ed* form (called the *past participle*—often irregular): **has** *departed,* **have** *cried,* **had** *seen.* They **have** *traveled* from near and far. She **had** not *heard* from him since their graduation.
- *Be (am, is, are . . .).* After these, the main verb uses its *-ing* form (called the *present participle*) or sometimes the *-ed* form (*past participle*):

  -ing form: **is** *flying,* **was** *dreaming.* The guests **are** *arriving* a few at a time. You **are** *driving* there, but I **am** *flying.*
  -ed form: **was** *divided,* **were** *stolen.* Traffic **was** *diverted* downtown. They **were** never *told* about him.

- *Do (does, did).* After these, the main verb keeps its original form: **do** *know,* **did** *play.* We **did** *call* you about that. I **do** not *care.*
- *Other auxiliaries* (*called* **modals**):

will, would	shall, should	may, might
can, could	have to	must
ought to	need (to)	dare (to)
used to		

After a modal, the main verb keeps its original form: **will** *go,* **could** *see,* **might** *disagree,* **would** *advise,* **has to** *pay,* **must** *return,* **ought to** *apologize.* The party **will** *begin* soon. I **might** not *stay* long. I **have to** *be* at work early tomorrow.

For more on *will* and *would,* see 116B, C, F, G, pages 10–11. For *used to,* see 116B, page 10.

A main verb may have up to three auxiliaries, combining the types above: Everyone **should be** *having* a good time. Nick and Sophie **must** certainly **have** *suspected* something. **Could** they **have been** *leading* us on?

115. The Principal Parts of Verbs

115A. Present, Past, and Past Participle. The three **principal parts** are the parts you need to know to form any of a verb's tenses (time forms):

Principal Part→	Present Tense	Past Tense	Past Participle
Regular verb	walk	walk**ed**	walk**ed**
Irregular verb	see	saw	seen

To form the past tense and past participle of regular verbs, just add *-ed* to the present tense: *stay, stayed, stayed*; attend, *attended, attended*. (Some regular verbs change their spelling slightly: *stop, stopped; cry, cried.*)

For irregular verbs, you need to learn their forms, such as *sing, sang, sung; break, broke, broken; think, thought, thought.* Section 115B lists the forms of many irregular verbs. Consult your dictionary for others. Do not assume that one irregular verb is like another: *make (made, made),* for instance, is formed differently from *take (took, taken).*

> *Note:* Some texts and dictionaries list as a fourth principal part the **present participle,** formed with *-ing* added to the present form: *seeing, playing.* Since it is always regular, except for some minor spelling changes *(stopping, loving),* there is no need to list it as a principal part in *English Simplified.*

115B. Some Troublesome Principal Parts. Here are the standard principal parts of some troublesome irregular verbs and a few regular ones. Asterisked verbs (*) are further explained in 404, pages 54–59.

ESL		
Present Tense	**Past Tense**	**Past Participle**
[be] am, is, are	was, were	been
begin	began	begun
blow	blew	blown
*break	broke	broken
*bring	brought	brought
choose	chose	chosen
(be)come	(be)came	(be)come
cost	cost	cost

Present Tense	**Past Tense**	**Past Participle**
dive	dived (preferred to *dove*)	dived
do	did	done
draw	drew	drawn
drink	drank	drunk
drive	drove	driven
fall	fell	fallen
fly	flew	flown
forbid	forbade, forbad	forbidden
freeze	froze	frozen
get	got	gotten, got
give	gave	given
go	went	gone
grow	grew	grown
know	knew	known
*lay [to put]	laid	laid
*lead [say "leed"]	led	led
*lie [to rest]	lay	lain
*lose	lost	lost
mean	meant	meant
pay	paid	paid
read [say "reed"]	read [say "red"]	read [say "red"]
ride	rode	ridden
ring	rang	rung
*(a)rise	(a)rose	(a)risen
run	ran	run
say	said	said
see	saw	seen
seek	sought	sought
shake	shook	shaken
shine [to give off light]	shone	shone
shine [to polish]	shined	shined
show	showed	shown, showed
sink	sank	sunk
sneak	sneaked [avoid *snuck*]	sneaked
speak	spoke	spoken
steal	stole	stolen

Present Tense	Past Tense	Past Participle
swear	swore	sworn
swim	swam	swum
swing	swung	swung
*take	took	taken
tear	tore	torn
think	thought	thought
throw	threw	thrown
(a)wake	(a)woke, (a)waked	(a)waked, (a)woke(n)
[*Awaken* is a different verb. It is regular.]		
wear	wore	worn
*write	wrote	written

116. Tense and Other Verb Forms.

ESL Tense refers to time: a verb uses different tense forms to show different times. You need to know only three endings to form all the tenses of regular verbs:

-s (sometimes **-es**)   **-ed** (sometimes **-d**)   **-ing**

Observe carefully where each ending occurs in the tense charts throughout section 116. Proofread your writing very carefully to be sure you never omit these endings.

The Three Simple Tenses

Each tense conveys a single time:

Present	Past	Future
walk(**s**) [regular verb]	walk**ed**	**will/shall** walk
see(**s**) [irregular verb]	saw	**will/shall** see

Note: Verb forms are often listed by **person,** as in the charts below. In grammar, there are three persons: The *first person* means the person(s) speaking: *I* or *we.* The *second person* means the person(s) being spoken to: *you.* The *third person* means the person(s) or thing(s) being spoken about: *he, she, it, they,* or any noun, such as *house, athletes, Horace.*

116A. The Present Tense

Basic form: first principal part. Notice the *-s* ending (arrow).

Person	Singular	Plural
1st	I walk	we walk
2nd	you walk	you walk
3rd	he/she/it walk**s**←	they walk

Uses:

(1) When something happens regularly or always: I usually *watch* the late news. Beth *drives* a minivan. The sun *sets* in the west.
(2) (Only with certain verbs: *be, have,* verbs of mental action, emotion, and the senses, such as *see, hear, think, understand, feel, know*) When something is happening at the present moment: I *am* ready. They *have* coffee. I *hear* a plane. She *understands* it. They *know* the way.

Most verbs use the *progressive* or *emphatic* form (see below) in questions and negatives.

Note: You may use the present when discussing a literary work, even though events are actually past: In chapter two Roger *runs* away with Cynthia. This act *exemplifies* the author's mastery of irony.

Progressive form: *am, is,* or *are* + *-ing* form

Person	Singular	Plural
1st	I **am** walk**ing**	we **are** walk**ing**
2nd	you **are** walk**ing**	you **are** walk**ing**
3rd	he/she/it **is** walk**ing**	they **are** walk**ing**

Use: To stress that something is in progress at the present moment: Right now I *am* [or *I'm*] *exercising.* She *is* [or *She's*] *traveling* today. **Questions and answers:** *Are* you *walking?* Yes, I *am* [*I'm*] *walking. Are* the Smiths *participating?* The Smiths *are participating.* **Negatives:** I *am* [*I'm*] not *walking.* The Smiths *are* not [*aren't*] *participating.*

Emphatic form: *do* or *does* + first principal part

Person	Singular	Plural
1st	I **do** walk	we **do** walk
2nd	you **do** walk	you **do** walk
3rd	he/she/it **does** walk	they **do** walk

Uses:

(1) To emphasize the verb: You never remember my birthday. Yes, I *do remember* it.
(2) In most questions and negatives (when you are not using the progressive): **Questions:** *Do* you *walk* regularly? *Does* she *care* for him? **Negatives:** I *do* not [*don't*] *walk.* She *does* not [*doesn't*] *care* for him. **Answers:** Answers to *yes–no* questions keep the emphatic form: *Do* you *smoke?* No, I *do* not [*don't*] *smoke.* Answers to other questions ordinarily use the basic form: Where *do* you *live?* I *live* in Ohio.

116B. The Past Tense

Basic form: second principal part. Notice the *-ed* ending on regular verbs.

Person	Singular	Plural
1st	I walk**ed** [regular], I saw [irregular]	we walk**ed**, saw
2nd	you walk**ed**, saw	you walk**ed**, saw
3rd	he/she/it walk**ed**, saw	they walk**ed**, saw

Use: When something was completed at a definite time in the past: I *walked* two miles yesterday. He *died* in 1826. I *attended* college for two years. They *tried* often and finally *succeeded*.

Progressive form: *was* or *were* + *-ing* form

Person	Singular	Plural
1st	I **was** walk**ing**	we **were** walk**ing**
2nd	you **were** walk**ing**	you **were** walk**ing**
3rd	he/she/it **was** walk**ing**	they **were** walk**ing**

Use: To stress that something was in progress at a time in the past: I *was walking* last night. She *was studying* when I called her. **Questions and answers:** *Were* you *walking?* Yes, I *was walking. Was* she *studying?* Yes, she *was studying*. **Negatives:** I *was* not [*wasn't*] *walking*. The Smiths *were* not [*weren't*] *participating*.

Emphatic form: *did* + first principal part

Person	Singular	Plural
1st	I **did** walk	we **did** walk
2nd	you **did** walk	you **did** walk
3rd	he/she/it **did** walk	they **did** walk

Uses:

(1) To emphasize the verb: Yes, I *did remember* your birthday.
(2) In most questions and negatives (when you are not using the progressive): **Questions:** *Did* you *walk* [yesterday or regularly]? Yes, I *did walk. Did* she *care* for him? Yes, she *did care.* **Negatives:** I *did* not [*did*n't] *walk*. She *did* not [*did*n't] *care* for him. **Answers:** Same rules as for present tense. See 116A.

Used to and ***would*** **forms** (notice the spelling: *used to*): Use these to show that something occurred repeatedly over a time in the past: At home I *used to sleep* late. She *used to write* often but no longer does. In the winters we *would* usually *go* skiing on Mount Mansfield, but Ed *would stay* home.

116C. The Future Tense

Basic form: *will* (or *shall*) + first principal part

> *Note:* In the U.S., *I shall* and *we shall* are considered very formal for expressing ordinary futurity. *Shall* can be used in all persons to convey determination or command: We *shall overcome*. They *shall* not *pass*.

Person	Singular	Plural
1st	I **shall/will** walk	we **shall/will** walk
2nd	you **will** walk	you **will** walk
3rd	he/she/it **will** walk	they **will** walk

Use: For future happenings: I *will* [*shall*] *walk* tomorrow. She *will study* just before the test. The Smiths *will participate. Will* you *walk* tomorrow? I *will* [*I'll*] *walk*.

Progressive form: *will* (or *shall*) *be* + *-ing* form

Person	Singular	Plural
1st	I **shall/will be** walk**ing**	we **shall/will be** walk**ing**
2nd	you **will be** walk**ing**	you **will be** walk**ing**
3rd	he/she/it **will be** walk**ing**	they **will be** walk**ing**

Use: To show that something will be in progress: I *will* [*shall*] *be leaving* soon. I'*ll be leaving* soon. She *will* [*She'll*] *be studying* when you call. *Will* she *be studying?* No, she *will* not [*won't*] *be studying*.

Going to **form:** *am, is,* or *are going to* + first principal part: I *am* [*I'm*] *going to walk*, you *are* [*you're*] *going to walk*, and so forth.

Uses:

(1) Same as basic future form: Tonight it'*s going to rain*.
(2) To stress intent: I'*m going to be* a ballet star.

> *Note:* At times you may use the present tense to express the future: The plane *leaves* at noon. Ron *is graduating* next year.

Emphatic form: None. Only the present and past tenses have this form.

The Three Perfect Tenses*

Each tense conveys a relation of two times:

Present Perfect	Past Perfect	Future Perfect
have/has walk**ed**	**had** walk**ed**	**will/shall have** walk**ed**
have/has seen	**had** seen	**will/shall have** seen

*Perfect here has its original meaning (from Latin) of "completed."

116D. The Present Perfect Tense

Basic form: *have* (or *has*) + third principal part

Person	Singular	Plural
1st	I **have** walk**ed**, I **have** seen	we **have** walked, seen
2nd	you **have** walk**ed**, seen	you **have** walk**ed**, seen
3rd	he/she/it **has** walk**ed**, seen	they **have** walk**ed**, seen

Uses: Generally,

(1) When something happened or began in the past but has some connection with the present: I *have* [*I've*] *walked* for hours [I am or may be still walking or have just finished walking]. She *has* [*She's*] *studied* since midnight. Ms. Stein *has lived* here forty years [lived here in the past and is still living here]. The FBI *has arrested* them [event is close to the present and affects the present].

(2) When something happened at some indefinite time up to the present: They *have threatened* a strike before [at some indefinite time].

Progressive form: *have* (or *has*) *been* + *-ing* form: I **have been** walk**ing,** you **have been** walk**ing,** and so forth.

Use: To stress that something has been and still is in progress: *Have* you *been walking?* I *have* [*I've*] *been walking* since noon. *Has* she *been thinking* about changing jobs? Yes, she *has* [*been thinking*].

116E. The Past Perfect Tense

Basic form: *had* + third principal part

Person	Singular	Plural
1st	I **had** walk**ed**	we **had** walk**ed**
2nd	you **had** walk**ed**	you **had** walk**ed**
3rd	he/she/it **had** walk**ed**	they **had** walk**ed**

Use: To clarify that something was completed before (or continued up to the time of) something else in the past: She *had walked* for hours before help came. Until I arrived with the car, she *had walked.* The witness said [yesterday] that she *had seen* the accident [last month]. Ella *had* already *divorced* Kurt when she met Max.

Progressive form: *had been* + *-ing* form: I *had been walking,* you *had been walking*, and so forth.

Use: To clarify that something was in progress before (or up to the time of) something else in the past: I *had been investing* heavily when the market collapsed. She *had been feeling* anxious before the wedding.

116F. The Future Perfect Tense

Basic form: *will* (or *shall*) *have* + third principal part

Person	Singular	Plural
1st	I **shall/will have** walk**ed**	we **shall/will have** walk**ed**
2nd	you **will have** walk**ed**	you **will have** walk**ed**
3rd	he/she/it **will have** walk**ed**	they **will have** walk**ed**

Use: When something will already be completed at a certain future time: They *will have escaped* [completed action] before the guards find out [future time—notice that this future event (*find*) takes the present tense]. By March [future], Stark *will* already *have left* office [completed action]. By the time I reach Phoenix, she *will have found* my letter.

Progressive form: *will* (or *shall*) *have been* + *-ing* form: I *shall/will have been walking,* you *will have been walking*, and so forth.

Use: To stress that something will already have been in progress at a future time: By midnight she *will have been studying* for fifteen hours nonstop. Next Monday he *will have been working* here a month.

> **Note:** Sometimes there is little difference in meaning between the basic and progressive perfect forms, and either will do: I *have waited* here since noon. I *have been waiting* here since noon.

116G. The Conditional Forms

The conditional: *would* + first principal part: I *would walk,* you *would walk*, and so forth.

Use: To express a possible future occurrence: If an asteroid struck Earth [in the future], we *would* all *die.* [Notice that the other verb, *struck,* uses the past tense.] If she ran for mayor, I *would vote* for her.

> **Note:** For a more immediate or likely condition, you may use the present tense and *will:* If that approaching asteroid strikes Earth, we *will* all *die.* If she runs for mayor, I *will vote* for her.

> **Note:** *Would* is used also in polite requests or questions: *Would* you please pass the artichokes. *Would* you like some cake? (See 207B, page 35, for punctuation of polite requests.) Still another use is with a repeated past action. See 116B, page 10.

The perfect conditional: *would have* + third principal part: I *would have walked,* you *would have walked*, and so forth.

Use: When a past condition did not actually occur: If an asteroid *had struck* Earth [it actually did not], we all *would have died.* [Notice that the other verb, *had struck,* uses the past perfect tense.] If she had run for mayor, I *would have voted* for her.

Cautions with the conditional forms:

Ordinarily, do not use *would* in both the *if* clause and the main clause:

> *Wrong:* If an asteroid *would have struck* Earth, we all *would have died.*
> *Right:* If an asteroid *had struck* Earth, we all *would have died.*

Avoid *would have liked to have . . .* :

> *Wrong:* They *would have liked* to *have seen* Paris.
> *Right:* They *would have liked* [in the past] to *see* Paris.
> They *would like* [now] to *have seen* Paris [in the past].
> They *would like* [now] to *see* Paris [in the future].

> *Note on verbs:* You will find other information on verbs elsewhere: **modals** in 114D, page 7; **voice** in 118C, page 13; **mood** in 118D, page 13; and **agreement** in 126, page 21.

117. Distinguishing Verbals from Verbs. When is a verb not a verb? When it is a verbal. A **verbal** is a form derived from a verb but used instead as a noun, adjective, or adverb. There are three kinds of verbals: **infinitives, participles,** and **gerunds.**

117A. The Infinitive (*to* + basic verb form), used as

A noun:

> *To act* is her ambition. [subject]
> She desires *to act.* [direct object]
> Her ambition is *to act.* [subject complement]

An adjective:

> Hers is an ambition *to admire.* [modifies *ambition*]

An adverb:

> Her goal is not easy *to attain.* [modifies *easy*]
> She came here *to study.* [modifies *came*]

> *Note:* The *to* is dropped after a very few verbs: *Let* them ~~to~~ go. We *made* them ~~to~~ leave. After *help,* either way is correct: We *helped* her [to] pack. **ESL**

117B. The Participle, used as an adjective:

Present participle (verb + *-ing*). In each example below, *laughing* modifies *children:*

> The *laughing* children brightened our spirits.
> The children, *laughing* at their play, brightened our spirits.
> *Laughing* at their play, the children brightened our spirits.

Past participle (third principal part of verb—see 115A, B, page 7). In the first three examples, *stunned* modifies *students:*

> The *stunned* students could not believe their grades.
> Completely *stunned,* the students could not believe their grades.
> The students, *stunned* by their grades, mobbed the professor.

In the following example, *chosen* modifies *woman:*

> All admired the woman *chosen* as their leader.

Use the *present* participle with a person or thing that is doing something: a *devastating* flood (the flood is doing the devastating). Use the *past* participle with a person or thing to which something has been done: the *devastated* land (the land has had devastation done to it).

117C. The Gerund (verb + *-ing*), used as a noun:

> *Seeing* [subject] is *believing* [subject complement].
> The prisoners considered *escaping* [direct object] by *tunneling* [object of preposition].

See 211C, page 36, for possessives with gerunds.

> *Note:* Whether an *–ing* verbal is a gerund or a participle depends on its use in a particular sentence:
> *Running* is excellent exercise. [gerund: used as subject noun]
> The *running* water soon turned cold. [participle: used as adjective, modifying *water*]

Infinitives, participles, and gerunds also have a *have* form for the earlier of two events: *To have worked* so hard exhausted him [infinitive]. *Having worked* hard for years, he was glad to retire [participle]. He was praised for *having worked* so hard [gerund].

118. Avoiding Verb Errors

118A. Use the Correct Perfect and Passive Forms. Remember that the perfect tenses (which take *have* as an auxiliary) need the past participle (third principal part), not the past tense (second principal part):

Wrong	Right
They *had went* earlier.	They *had* **gone** earlier.
I *have* just *began* to write.	I *have* just **begun** to write.
Robbers *had broke* the window.	Robbers *had* **broken** the window.
He *has ran* a mile every day.	He *has* **run** a mile every day.
We *would have froze* if you *had*n't *came* along.	We *would have* **frozen** if you *had*n't **come** along.
You *should have took* the earlier bus.	You *should have* **taken** the earlier bus.

The same is true for the passive voice (which uses *be* as an auxiliary—see 118C for an explanation of passive voice):

Wrong	Right
Lori *is shook* up by the news.	Lori *is* **shaken** up by the news.
Some wine *was drank* that night.	Some wine *was* **drunk** that night.
The bell *had been rang* twice.	The bell *had been* **rung** twice.
My car *was stole* last night.	My car *was* **stolen** last night.

118B. Do Not Shift Tense Without Reason.

Wrong: In the film a Dominican family *immigrates* [present tense] to New York but *found* [past tense] life difficult there.

Right: In the film a Dominican family *immigrates* to New York but *finds* life difficult there. [both verbs in present tense]

Right: In the film a Dominican family *immigrated* to New York but *found* life difficult there. [both verbs in past tense]

118C. Do Not Overuse the Passive Voice.
Transitive verbs have two voices: **active** and **passive.** The verb forms you learned in sections 116A–G are all in the active voice, which is the more common one. We form the passive voice with *be* (*am, is, are, was, were . . .*) + the past participle (third principal part)—for example, *was made, are shined, will be driven:*

Active voice: Action goes from subject (the doer) (→) to direct object (the receiver).	Passive voice: Subject becomes the receiver (←) of the action. The doer is in a *by* phrase or omitted.
The Republicans (→) *nominated* Nora Stern.	Nora Stern (←) *was nominated* [by the Republicans].
Miller now *leads* the orchestra.	The orchestra *is* now *led* by Miller.
Alice Walker *will read* the poem.	The poem *will be read* by Alice Walker.
The Dolphins *could have won* the game.	The game *could have been won* [by the Dolphins].

In general, the active voice, which stresses the doer, is more forceful than the passive, which stresses the receiver. Use the active voice unless you have a specific reason for using the passive (see below).

To make a passive sentence active, ask, "Who (or what) is doing the action?" Use the answer as your subject. In both sentences below, Tyrone Willingham is doing the action:

Passive: The story *was written* by **Tyrone Willingham.**
Active: **Tyrone Willingham** *wrote* the story.

Use the passive only when

Your emphasis is on the receiver: The senator *has been punched* by an irate taxpayer. [The focus is on the senator, not the puncher.]

The doer is unimportant: The package *will be delivered* soon. [The deliverer's name is unimportant.]

The doer is unknown: Their car *was stolen* from the driveway.

You want to deemphasize or conceal the doer: Yes, an error *has been made* at this office. [The person who committed the error is not named.]

See 130D, page 29, on voice consistency.

118D. Use the Subjunctive Correctly.
The **subjunctive** form of a verb expresses doubt, uncertainty, wish, or supposition, or signals a condition contrary to fact. In the subjunctive, some verb forms change:

Am, is, and *are* change to *be.*
Was changes to *were.*
Has changes to *have.*
All other verbs drop their *-s* form: *lives* becomes *live, goes* becomes *go. . . .*

Wish: God *be* with you. Long *live* the queen. Far *be* it from me to interfere in his life. My wish is that she *have* a happy marriage.

Doubt or uncertainty: If I *were* to tell him, he might tell everyone.

Condition contrary to fact: If I *were* you, I would tell. He struts around as if he *were* king of the world.

Also, use the subjunctive in a *that* clause when the main clause expresses a demand, command, recommendation, request, or parliamentary motion:

They demanded that the store *refund* their money.
The board recommends that the treasurer *resign* at once.
I move that the meeting *be* adjourned.

Note: The subjunctive is one of three **moods.** The others are called the *indicative* (statements and questions) and the *imperative* (commands and requests). There are no special forms for these two moods, except for imperative *be:* Be quiet. See 103A, page 2, for examples.

118E. Do Not Confuse Verbs Similar in Meaning or Spelling.
If similar verbs, such as *lie* and *lay,* confuse you, try mentally substituting a synonym, such as *rest* for *lie* and *put* for *lay.* Many sets of troublesome verbs, such as *lie/lay* and *raise/rise,* are explained in 404, pages 54–59.

For resources to help you master this section's topics, log in to www.mywritinglab.com and select Verbs, Tense, and Regular and Irregular Verbs from the list of subtopics.

119–120. Using Adjectives and Adverbs

Recall that an adjective modifies (describes or limits) a noun or occasionally a pronoun, and that an adverb modifies a verb or sometimes an adjective or another adverb:

Adjectives: [descriptive] a *blue* shirt, a *long* game, a *subterranean* chamber, a *hefty* textbook; [limiting] *this* shirt, *seven* games, *some* textbooks

Adverbs: The guitarist performed *admirably* [modifying a verb, *performed*]. The guitarist was *quite* talented [modifying an adjective, *talented*]. The guitarist performed *quite* admirably [modifying an adverb, *admirably*].

To form most adverbs, add *-ly* to the adjective:

smooth → smooth**ly**   regrettable → regrettab**ly**
delightful → delightful**ly**   easy → easi**ly**

Thus a word with an *-ly* ending is usually an adverb—but not always: *friendly, womanly,* and *saintly,* for example, are adjectives. Also, some adverbs have the same form as their corresponding adjectives (*late, early, fast . . .*), and some have two forms (*slow[ly], quick[ly] . . .*). The sure way to tell adverbs and adjectives apart is to determine the word that is modified:

> You drive too *fast.* [drive how? *Fast* = adverb.]
> You are in the *fast* lane. [which lane? *Fast* = adjective.]

The word *not* is an adverb.

119. Using Adjectives and Adverbs Correctly

119A. Use an Adverb (Not an Adjective)

To modify an action verb:
> ***Wrong:*** The team played *careless* today.
> ***Right:*** The team played *carelessly* today.

To modify an adjective:
> ***Wrong:*** The political speaker's comments were *real* outrageous.
> ***Right:*** The political speaker's comments were *really* outrageous.

> ***Wrong:*** We had *extreme* slow service at McBurger's.
> ***Right:*** We had *extremely* slow service at McBurger's.

To modify another adverb:
> ***Wrong:*** Tamara tries *awful* hard.
> ***Right:*** Tamara tries *awfully* [better, *quite*] hard.

119B. Use an Adjective After a Linking Verb (as a subject complement):
> The weather was *dismal.* [*Dismal* describes *weather.*]
> Our tiny room smelled *damp.* [*Damp* describes *room.*]

See 114C, page 7, for more on linking verbs.

119C. Use *good* and *well, bad* and *badly* Correctly. Use *good* and *bad* (adjectives) after a linking verb (as subject complements):
> They are quite *good.* I feel *good.* This fish tastes *bad.*

Use *well* and *badly* (adverbs) to modify an action verb:
> She sings *well.* I have failed *badly.*

> *Note: Well* can be an adjective when it means "in good health": I am feeling *well.* She is not a *well* woman. *I feel good,* on the other hand, refers to any kind of good feeling, such as from winning a race.

119D. Use Comparative and Superlative Forms Correctly. **Most adjectives and adverbs have three degrees**. Notice how the *-er* and *-est* endings change the degree:

> ***Positive (modifying one thing or action):*** Cheryl is a *fast* runner and should finish *early.*

> ***Comparative (comparing two):*** Cheryl is a *faster* runner than Mia and should finish *earlier.*
> ***Superlative (comparing three or more):*** Cheryl is the *fastest* of all the runners and should finish *earliest.*

Some comparisons use *more* or *most.* Most long adjectives and most adverbs use *more* and *most* instead of *-er* and *-est: fanciful, more fanciful, most fanciful; smoothly, more smoothly, most smoothly.* Some adjectives and adverbs use either form: *costlier, costliest* or *more costly, most costly.* (To express the opposite of *more* and *most,* use *less* and *least: less smoothly, least smoothly.*)

A few adjectives and adverbs have irregular forms of comparison:

| good/well, better, best | many/much, more, most |
| bad/badly, worse, worst | little, less, least |

Use the comparative (not the superlative) when comparing two things:
> ***Wrong:*** Lee is the *smallest* of the twins.
> ***Right:*** Lee is the *smaller* of the twins.

Do not use double comparatives (both *more* and *-er*) or superlatives (both *most* and *-est*). One form is enough:
> ***Wrong:*** This beam is *more stronger* than the other.
> ***Right:*** This beam is *stronger* than the other.

> ***Wrong:*** She is the *most unlikeliest* of heroes.
> ***Right:*** She is the *unlikeliest* [or the *most unlikely*] of heroes.

Do not compare adjectives that cannot logically be compared, such as *unique, fatal, impossible, square, empty.* A task is either possible or impossible; it cannot be more (or less) impossible. Instead, say *more nearly impossible* or *closer to impossible:*

> ***Wrong:*** Gehry's new museum is *more unique* than any built previously.
> ***Right:*** Gehry's new museum is *more innovative* [*more original, closer to unique . . .*] than any built previously.

Likewise, such words cannot be modified by an adverb of degree: ~~very~~ unique, ~~extremely~~ fatal.

120. Using Articles and Determiners `ESL` Correctly

120A. Choosing *a* or *an.* Before a vowel sound (*a, e, i, o, u,* sometimes *y*), use *an: an* accident, *an* image, *an* honest person (*h* is silent), *an* uncle, *an* FBI (eff-bee-eye) agent, *an* A, *an* $80 (eighty-dollar) check.

Before a consonant (any nonvowel) sound, use *a: a* car, *a* mystery, *a* university (*u* pronounced as consonant *y* + *u: yu*), *a* young child (consonant *y*), *a* D, *a* $70 (seventy-dollar) check.

120B. Using Articles with Different Kinds of Nouns. With any noun, you need to know whether to use (1) *a/an*—called the **indefinite article,** (2) *the*—called the **definite article,** or (3) no article at all. First, learn these definitions:

A **count noun** is one that can be counted, such as *car:* one car, two cars, three cars, several cars . . . ; one reason, two reasons, many reasons. . . .

A **noncount noun** cannot be counted: *health* (we do not say *one health, two healths, many healths*), *courage, gold.* Noncount nouns include concepts and qualities *(truth, honesty),* emotions *(sadness),* activities *(swimming),* substances *(methane, milk),* school subjects *(chemistry),* and other things considered in bulk or mass *(baggage, underwear, wheat).*

Certain nouns are sometimes noncount (I felt *joy*) and sometimes count (the *joys* of youth).

A **familiar term** is one that the reader already knows; the writer may have mentioned it already or may explain it immediately, or it may be in the reader's prior knowledge (such as the campus library).

An **unfamiliar** term is the opposite: the writer has not previously mentioned it or does not immediately explain it, nor is it in the reader's prior knowledge (a faraway library, any library).

Rules for Using **a(n),** *the, or No Article*

Before—	Use—	Example
COUNT NOUNS Unfamiliar singular	*a* or *an*	*An* [any] accident *victim* needs *a* [any] good *lawyer. A bus* has skidded into *a tree.* [Reader has not known about the bus or tree before.] Ames is *a city* in Iowa. [one of many cities in Iowa]
Unfamiliar plural	[no article]	*Fires* broke out in Florida. [Reader has not known of these before.] *Victims* [any victims] need *lawyers* promptly.
Familiar (singular or plural)	*the*	[If victim and lawyer are already known or have been mentioned] *The victim* should see *the lawyer* promptly. *The war* is over. *The stars* are out.
NONCOUNT NOUNS	[usually no article]	*Peace* is near. She prefers *wine.* They fought with *honor.* He felt *embarrassment.*
SUPERLATIVES	*the*	*the* most fearful child, *the* highest ratings
PROPER NOUNS Singular naming a ship, body of water (except lake or bay), organization, personal title, or structure	*the*	*the* Titanic, *the* Nile, *the* Arctic Ocean, *the* Senate, *the* Duke of York, *the* President, *the* Sears Tower, *the* Statue of Liberty

Before—	Use—	Example
All other singular	[no article]	Australia, Lake Mead, Bard College, Queen Victoria, Sally Stetson
Plural	*the*	*the* Great Lakes, *the* Smiths, *the* Dodgers

The above rules are just the basics. To master English articles, notice their use in your reading and listen closely to native English speakers around you and on television.

120C. Using Limiting Adjectives (Determiners)

Before—	Use (with example)—
COUNT NOUNS Singular	*one* day, *every* way, *each* new clerk, *either* person, *another* problem, the *other* day, *such* a day, *enough* tea
Plural	*many* flights, *most* days, [a] *few* new ideas, *all* [the] cars, *other* people, *such* hats, *both* nations, *enough* apples, *some* players, *more* students
NONCOUNT NOUNS	[the] *most* rain, *all* humankind, *other* equipment, *such* joy, *more* wine, *enough* trouble, [a] *little* time, *some* sugar

For more on determiners, see 106A, page 3.

120D. Putting Articles, Determiners, and Other Adjectives in Order. Before a noun, place adjectives in this order, from the beginning:

> ***First***—articles, determiners, and possessive nouns or pronouns: *the, some, my, Janet's* [*my* friends]
> ***Second***—numbers: *five, fifth* [my *five* friends]
> ***Third***—descriptive adjectives: *enormous, round, old, silver, cranky* [my five *old* friends]
> ***Fourth***—nouns used as adjectives: *car* wheels, *bank* loans, *elephant* tusks [my five old *college* friends]

For resources to help you master this section's topics, log in to www.mywritinglab.com and select Adjectives ***and*** Adverbs ***from the list of subtopics.***

121–123. Using Pronouns

A pronoun substitutes for a noun, so that instead of saying *The ambassador announced that* **the ambassador** *would make* **the ambassador's** *first trip to Slovenia,* we can say *The ambassador announced that* **she** *would make* **her** *first trip to Slovenia.*

The noun that the pronoun substitutes for (stands for) is called its **antecedent.** In the second example above, *ambassador* is the antecedent of *she* and *her.* (Not all kinds of pronouns have expressed antecedents.)

Pronouns share almost all the uses of nouns. To review those uses, see 112, page 5.

121. The Kinds of Pronouns

121A. The Personal Pronouns. These designate one or more particular persons or things:

Person	Singular	Plural
FIRST [person(s) speaking]	I, my, mine, me	we, our, ours, us
SECOND [person(s) spoken to]	you, your, yours	you, your, yours
THIRD [any other person(s) or thing(s)]	he, his, him, she, her, hers, it, its	they, their, theirs, them

The gender problem. Avoid using *he, his,* or *him* in contexts applicable to both sexes:

> **Considered sexist:** It is difficult for a teenager to select a career that will satisfy *him*. Every student needs *his* identification card. [But half of teenagers and students are female.]

Substituting for *he, his,* and *him* presents a problem because English lacks common-gender equivalents of these words. Try either of the following solutions, taking care to preserve clarity and consistency with context:

> **Shift to the plural where possible:** It is difficult for *teenagers* to select careers that will satisfy *them*. All *students* need *their* identification cards.

> **Remove gender where possible:** A teenager finds it difficult selecting a satisfying career. Student identification cards are required. A worker's attitude affects ~~his~~ job performance.

Other solutions are less satisfactory. Using *he or she, his or her, her or him* (every student needs *his or her* identification card) sounds clumsy, especially after several repetitions. Substituting *you* or *your* to mean *everyone* or *anyone* (In this college *you* find it difficult selecting a satisfying career) can be too informal. Using *they, their,* or *them* with a singular antecedent (every *student* needs *their* identification card) violates grammatical logic (though many reputable writers consider it acceptable as *notional* agreement; that is, by considering that the sense of words such as *everyone, anyone,* or *every student* is plural).

121B. The Interrogative and Relative Pronouns

The interrogative pronouns include *who (whose, whom), which,* and *what.* They ask questions:

> *Who* saw the game? *Whose* team won? *What* was the score? *Which* of the players scored the most points? To *whom* was the trophy given?

The relative pronouns include *who (whose, whom), which,* and *that.* These basic relative pronouns introduce certain dependent clauses:

> Students *who live at home* save money.
> Maine, *which has a rugged coastline,* is a tourist favorite.
> I tore up the bill *that came in the mail.*

Another kind of relative pronoun—including *what, whoever (whomever, whosever), whichever,* and *whatever*—introduces certain other dependent clauses:

> Sheila reads *whatever comes in the mail.*

Who vs. which. Use *who* for persons, *which* for things, and *that* for either:

> **Person:** Students *who* (or *that*) use the dining hall must have meal cards.
> **Thing:** Tonight's meal is fajitas, *which* I enjoy. A meal *that* I enjoy is fajitas.

> *Note:* When *of which* sounds awkward, you may use *whose* with things: Venice is a city *whose* traffic jams are confined to waterways.

121C. The Demonstrative Pronouns are *this* (plural: *these*) and *that* (plural: *those*). They point out:

> *This* is your chance. All of *these* look good.
> You should buy *that. Those* are the best.

121D. The Indefinite Pronouns refer to no particular person or thing:

Number	Indefinite Pronouns
Singular	another, anybody, anyone, anything, each, either, everybody, everyone, everything, neither, nobody, no one, nothing, one, other, somebody, someone, something
Plural	both, few, many, others, several
Singular or Plural	all, any, more, most, none, some, such

> *Many* will complain, but *few* will act; *most* will do nothing.
> *Someone* must do *something,* but *no one* wants to do *anything.*
> *All* are welcome. *Each* of the houses is vacant.

> *Note:* Closely related to the indefinite pronouns are the two **reciprocal** pronouns, *each other* and *one another.* See 404, page 56.

121E. The Reflexive and Intensive Pronouns are the *-self* forms of personal pronouns: *myself, yourself, yourselves, himself, herself, itself, ourselves, themselves.*

They are called reflexive when used as objects or complements:

> This dishwasher shuts *itself* off. [direct object]
> The senators voted higher pay for *themselves.* [object of preposition]
> Just be *yourself.* [subject complement]

They are called intensive when used as appositives, for emphasis:

> He *himself* lost the cash. They *themselves* lost the cash.

Do not use a *-self* pronoun where a personal pronoun suffices:

> *Wrong:* The message was for Pat and *myself.*
> *Right:* The message was for Pat and *me.*

Caution: There are no such words in standard English as *hisself, ourself(s), yourselfs, theirself(s), theirselves, themself(s).*

122. Using the Right Case.

The **case** of a pronoun refers to the form it takes in a particular use in a sentence (subject, direct object, and so forth). English has three cases: **subjective** (nominative), **possessive,** and **objective.** Notice how most pronouns in the chart change their form according to their case:

	Subjective (Nominative) Case	Possessive Case	Objective Case
Singular	I	my, mine	me
	he, she, it	his, her, hers, its	him, her, it
Plural	we	our, ours	us
	they	their, theirs	them
Singular or Plural	you	your, yours	you
	who	whose	whom

The pronouns with different subjective and objective forms cause the most problems: *I/me, he/him, she/her, we/us, they/them, who/whom.*

122A. The Subjective (Nominative) Case. Use only the subjective forms (*I, he, she, we, they, who*) for a

> **Subject:** *I* know it. *He* and *I* know it. *Who* knows it? *They* know it.
> **Subject complement** (after linking verbs): The only one invited was *I.*

> *Note:* Although *It was her, It wasn't me,* and so forth are common in informal usage, most careful writers and speakers adhere to the subjective case in formal usage: It was *she.* It was not *he.* If a sentence such as *The only one invited was I* sounds awkward, you can recast it: *I was the only one invited.* (See the second 122C note below for pronoun case with the infinitive *to be.*)

122B. The Objective Case. Use only the objective forms (*me, him, her, us, them, whom*) for any kind of object:

> **Direct object:** State College has accepted *him.*
> **Indirect object:** Jan sent *her* and *me* invitations.
> **Object of preposition:** He told the details to *us.*

122C. Special Concerns with Subjective and Objective Cases. (For *who* and *whom,* see 122 D and E.)

A pronoun in a compound (with *and, or, but*) takes the same case as it would if not compounded:

> *Wrong: Him* and *me* can go. [Would you say *Him* can go, or *Me* can go?]
> *Right: He* and *I* can go. [*He* can go. *I* can go.]

> *Wrong:* Dad bought tickets for Max and *I.* [for *I?*]
> *Right:* Dad bought tickets for Max and *me.* [for *me*]

> *Note: Max and myself* is also wrong. See 121E, page 16.

> *Wrong:* Between *you* and *I* there should be no secrets.
> *Right:* Between *you* and *me* there should be no secrets.

A pronoun followed by a noun appositive takes the same case as it would without the noun (*appositive* is defined in 112D, page 6):

> *Wrong: Us* freshmen need guidance. [*Us* need?]
> *Right: We* freshmen need guidance. [*We* need]
> *Right:* The college offers guidance to *us* freshmen. [to *us*]

A pronoun appositive takes the same case as the word to which it is in apposition:

> *Subjective case:* Two *students, you* and *she,* will share the prize.
> *Objective case:* Professor Hunt told *us*—Len and *me*—to share the prize.
> *Objective case:* Let's [Let *us*] *you* and *me* try the bookstore.

A pronoun in an incomplete comparison takes the same case as if the comparison were complete. Notice the difference in meaning between these sentences:

> *Right:* She liked Pat more than *I.* [than I did]
> *Right:* She liked Pat more than *me.* [than she liked me]

For more on incomplete comparisons, see 130C, page 29.

> *Note:* For a pronoun between a verb and an infinitive (called the **subject of the infinitive**), use the objective case: She ordered *him* to leave. After *to be,* always use the same case as you do before it: The police thought *me* to be *her.*

> *Note:* Avoid unnecessary use of pronouns:
> *Unnecessary* he: In *Joyce's* famous story "The Dead," *he* uses snow as a symbol.
> *Better:* Joyce's famous story "The Dead" uses snow as a symbol.

122D. *Who* and *Whom* as Interrogative Pronouns. *Who* is subjective case; *whom* is objective:

> *Who* voted against the child-support law? [subject]
> *Whom* can the people blame? → The people can blame *whom?* [direct object]
> *Whom* can people appeal to? → To *whom* can people appeal? [object of preposition]

Note: When in doubt about using *who* or *whom*, try mentally substituting *he* or *him*. If *he* sounds right, use *who;* if *him* sounds right, use *whom:*

> (*Who/Whom*) rang the bell? → *He* rang the bell. → *Who* rang the bell?
>
> (*Who/Whom*) did you see? → You did see *him*. → You did see *whom?* → *Whom* did you see?

Although using *who* as an object is common in informal usage (*Who* did you see? *Who* did you go with?), formal usage requires *who* for subjects only, *whom* for objects: *Whom* did you see?

Directly after a preposition, use *whom:* With *whom* did you go? By *whom* was this written? (Exception: if a clause follows the preposition, *whoever* may be its subject: Give this to *whoever answers the doorbell* [not *whomever*—see 122E].)

122E. Who and ~~Whom~~ as Relative Pronouns. The case of a relative pronoun is determined by its use *within* its clause (for full explanation of clauses, see 125, page 20):

> Binoy is the one **who** *wrote the article.* [*Who* = subject of *wrote.*]
> Binoy is the one **whom** *we should consult.* [→ *we should consult* **whom**. *Whom* = direct object of *should consult.*]
> We should also consult **whoever** *collaborated* with him. [*Whoever* = subject of *collaborated.*]
> We should consult **whomever** *we can locate.* [→ *we can locate* **whomever**. *Whomever* = direct object of *locate.*]
> Send a letter to **whoever** *worked with Binoy.* [*Whoever* = subject of *worked.*]

Do not be misled by other intervening clauses, such as *I think, it seems,* or *we are convinced:*

> Binoy is the one **who** ⟨I think⟩ *wrote the article.*
> Binoy is the one **whom** ⟨it seems⟩ *we should consult.*

122F. The Possessive Case

Use an apostrophe ['] to form the possessive case of indefinite and reciprocal pronouns: *someone's, everybody's, no one's, anyone else's, somebody else's, each other's. . . .*

But never use an apostrophe in the possessive case of personal pronouns (*his, hers, its, ours, yours, theirs*) or of *who* (*whose*): *Whose* book is this? Is it *ours* or *theirs?* It can't be *hers.*

It is a common error to confuse the possessives *its, whose, their,* and *your* with the contractions *it's, who's, they're,* and *you're.*

Possessive Pronouns (never take apostrophe)	Contractions (always take apostrophe)
its [belonging to it]	it's [it is]
their [belonging to them]	they're [they are]
your [belonging to you]	you're [you are]
whose [belonging to whom]	who's [who is]

The store lost *its* license. *Whose* fault was that?
The stores lost *their* licenses. Was *your* store included?

To tell which form you need, mentally substitute the uncontracted form (*it is,* etc.). If that sounds right, you need the contraction:

> (*Its/It's*) too late now. → *It is* too late now. → *It's* too late now.
>
> The lion bared (*its/it's*) teeth. → The lion bared *it is* teeth? No. → The lion bared *its* teeth.

Use a possessive pronoun before a gerund:

> **Wrong:** We resented *him* leaving.
> **Right:** We resented *his* leaving.

See 211C, page 36, for more on possessives with gerunds.

Note: As you may have realized, many possessive pronouns serve also as adjectives: *his* house, *our* dinner, *their* grades. So do demonstrative and interrogative pronouns: *that* car, *whose* glasses, *which* game.

123. Avoiding Unclear Reference. Be sure that each pronoun clearly refers only to the one noun it stands for—its antecedent. Confusion occurs when a pronoun may refer to either of two (or more) antecedents or when there is no clear antecedent at all. Rephrase the sentence or supply a missing antecedent:

> **Unclear:** Ms. Tash told Ms. Romano that *she* was next. [Who was next?]
> **Clear:** Ms. Tash told Ms. Romano, "I'm next."
> **Clear:** Ms. Tash told Ms. Romano, "You're next."

> **Unclear:** . . . West of the bridge, *they* are developing another section of the rail trail. [*They* has no antecedent, either in this sentence or in preceding ones. Who are *they?*]
> **Clear:** West of the bridge, *the Parks Department* is developing another section of the rail trail.

It is acceptable, though, in *It is raining, It is your turn,* and so on.

> **Unclear:** This rug will not match our living-room furniture because *it* is too modern. [To what does *it* refer? Which is too modern—the rug or the furniture?]

> **Clear:** This rug, *which* is too modern, will not match our living-room furniture.
> **Clear:** This rug will not match our living-room furniture, *which* is too modern.

> **Unclear:** Everyone heard her response to his comment, *which* was uncalled for. [Was the comment uncalled for, or the response?]
> **Clear:** Everyone heard her uncalled-for response to his comment.
> **Clear:** Everyone heard her response to his uncalled-for comment.

Avoid using *which, it, this,* or *that* to refer to a whole phrase, clause, or sentence in an unclear way:

> **Unclear:** Acid rain is still a problem in the Northeast, resulting in increased support for a stronger antipollution law in Congress. What will happen because of *this* is uncertain.
>
> **Clear:** . . . What will happen because of *this new support* is uncertain.
>
> **Clear:** . . . What will happen because of *this continued pollution* is uncertain.
>
> **Unclear:** Officer Marchi decided to disobey the captain's order. *It* was a foolish thing. [Was the order foolish, or the disobeying?]
>
> **Clear:** Officer Marchi decided to disobey the captain's *foolish order.*
>
> **Clear:** Officer Marchi *foolishly decided* to disobey the captain's order.
>
> **Unclear:** The soprano Maria Faustina has cultivated a glamorous image that initially led many to question her seriousness as a person and an artist. Of *that* there can be no doubt. [Of what can there be no doubt?]
>
> **Clear:** There can be no doubt that the soprano Maria Faustina has cultivated *a glamorous image* that initially led many to question her seriousness as a person and an artist.
>
> **Clear (another meaning):** There is no doubt of Maria Faustina's *seriousness* as a person and an artist, though the glamorous image that she has cultivated led many initially to question that seriousness.
>
> **Unclear:** Profits are down in three of four categories. Production is being curtailed, and hundreds of workers are being laid off. Our advertising budget is being slashed. So far we have no solution for *it.*
>
> **Clear:** . . . So far we have no solution for *these problems.*

Do not use an adjective as an antecedent:

> **Wrong:** I stopped at a *soda* store and had *one.* [*Soda* is an adjective here, modifying *store.* The only noun is *store,* and the pronoun *one* clearly does not refer to *store.*]
>
> **Right:** I stopped at a *store* and had a *soda.*
>
> **Right:** I stopped at a *soda store* and had a *root beer.*

For resources to help you master this section's topics, log in to www.mywritinglab.com and select** Pronouns, Pronoun Case, **and** Pronoun References and Point of View **from the list of subtopics.

124–125. Recognizing Phrases and Clauses

Being able to recognize phrases and clauses is a key to good writing. It helps you compose clear, effective sentences and avoid many serious errors in agreement and sentence structure.

124. Phrases. A **phrase** is a group of related words that is less than a sentence, because it lacks a full verb. (Some phrases include part of a verb—see 124B.) In a sentence, a phrase functions as a single word (usually an adjective, adverb, or noun); for example, The car sped **away** [adverb].

The car sped **down the street** [adverb phrase]. Recognize and regard phrases as units.

> *Note:* Never write a phrase as if it were a complete sentence:
> **Wrong:** *In the shower.*
> **Right:** I sing *in the shower.*
>
> See Fragments, section 129A, page 26.

There are two main kinds of phrases:

124A. The Prepositional Phrase is used chiefly as an adjective or adverb. It consists of preposition + object (and perhaps modifiers of that object):

> **As adjective:** Apples *of Washington State* are especially delicious. [tells which apples]
> Charlie bought a drill *with a variable-speed control.* [tells what kind of drill]
> **As adverb:** They rode home *on their bicycles* [tells how] *after the show* [tells when].
> I bought it *for a birthday gift.* [tells why]

See 107B, page 4, for a list of prepositions.

124B. The Verbal Phrase. There are three kinds: infinitive, participial, and gerund. (See 117, page 12, for an explanation of these terms.)

An infinitive phrase (infinitive + completer or modifiers or both):

> **As noun:** *To win the trophy* is their aim. [subject]
> They want *to win the trophy.* [direct object]
> **As adjective:** I have a plan *to suggest to you.* [modifies *plan*]
> **As adverb:** We booked the trip early *to obtain the lowest rates.* [modifies *booked*—tells *why*]
> Darryl is eager *to leave soon.* [modifies *eager*]

A participial phrase (present participle [*-ing* form] or past participle [*-ed* form] + completer or modifiers or both) is always used as an adjective. It may come either before or after the noun it modifies:

> Students *needing extra credits* can enroll in Whiffleball 101. [present participial phrase, modifying *students*]
> *Exhausted from his all-night studies,* Carl stumbled into the examination room. [past participial phrase, modifying *Carl*]

Another kind of phrase using a participle is the **absolute phrase,** in which the participle has its own subject:

> *Her heart pounding wildly,* Karen rose to speak. [*Heart* is the subject of the participle *pounding.*]
> Karen rose to speak, *her heart pounding wildly.*

Sometimes *being* or a similar participle is omitted:

> *Her voice now a mere whisper,* Sueanne kept cheering. [that is, *Her voice now being a mere whisper* or *having become a mere whisper*]

A **gerund phrase** (*-ing* form + completer or modifiers or both) is always used as a noun:

> *Reducing the deficit substantially* must involve every level of government. [subject]
>
> The speaker stressed *reducing the deficit.* [direct object]
>
> What can we do about *reducing the deficit?* [object of preposition]
>
> Her chief concern is *reducing the deficit.* [subject complement]

For avoiding dangling or misplaced phrases, see 130B, page 28.

> **Note—Other Kinds of Phrases:** Some authorities use the term **noun phrase** to refer to a noun and its modifiers (*our varsity players in their new uniforms*) and **verb phrase** for a main verb and its auxiliaries (*should have been practicing*).

125. Clauses.
A **clause** is a group of related words containing subject + verb (see 103B, page 2). There are two kinds: **independent** (**main**) and **dependent** (**subordinate**).

125A. Kinds of Clauses **An independent clause** sounds complete and makes sense when it stands alone. Every simple sentence is an independent clause. As you learned in 103B (page 2), we can have two (or more) such clauses in a sentence:

Independent clause   *Independent clause*

The *virus began* to spread, and *doctors grew* alarmed.
Their *vaccine was* gone, but *they hoped* for more soon.

Independent clauses are normally connected by *and, but, yet, or, nor, for,* or *so* (a coordinating conjunction) or a semicolon (;). The conjunction is not considered part of either clause.

A dependent clause does not sound complete and does not make full sense when it stands alone—even though it has subject + verb. It contains a connecting word (such as *when, that,* or *if*) that requires the dependent clause to be attached to an independent clause:

Dependent clause

You may graduate **when** *you pay* your library fines.
The first topic **that** *Eva chose* for her paper was rejected.
If the *track is* slick, the Daytona 500 race can become dangerous.
We will appreciate **whatever** *you can do*.

> **Note:** Never write a dependent clause alone, as if it were a complete sentence.
>
> **Wrong:** *If you drive.*
> **Right:** *If you drive,* I can nap.
>
> See Fragments, section 129A, page 26.

In dependent clauses (unlike independent clauses), the connecting word is in most cases considered part of the clause.

125B. Kinds of Dependent Clauses ESL
Dependent clauses are used as **adjectives, adverbs,** or **nouns.**

An **adjective clause** (also called a **relative clause**) is used as an adjective, modifying a preceding noun or pronoun. It is introduced and connected to the independent clause by the relative pronoun *who (whose, whom), which,* or *that,* or by *when* or *where* (called a *relative adverb*):

> The book puzzled readers *who only skimmed it.* [modifies *readers*]
>
> The paperback edition, *which is selling briskly,* may soon be out of stock. [modifies *edition*]
>
> Books *that discuss the future* usually sell well. [modifies *books*]
>
> This is the season *when such books are popular.* [modifies *season*]

> **Note:** Sometimes you may omit the relative pronoun: The people ~~that~~ we met were friendly. But doing so may damage clarity. In most formal writing, it is better to keep the pronoun. (See 130C, page 29.)

For punctuation of adjective clauses, see 201F, page 32.

An **adverb clause** is used as an adverb—modifying a verb, adjective, or other adverb. It tells *how, when, where, why, with what result, under* or *despite what condition,* or *to what degree.* It is introduced and connected to the independent clause by a subordinating conjunction, such as the ones listed below.

Adverb Clause Telling—	Introduced by Subordinating Conjunction—	Example
Time [*when?*]	when(ever), while, after, before, since, as, as soon as, until	I finished the test *before time expired.*
Place [*where?*]	where, wherever	We followed the trail *wherever it led.*
Manner [*how?*]	as, as if, as though	He acts *as if he's in charge.*
Cause [*why?*]	because, since	The party was dull *because few people came.*
Purpose [*why?*]	(so) that, in order that	She woke early *so that she could study more.*
Condition [*under what condition?*]	if, unless, whether, provided	You will be drenched *if you forget your raincoat.*
Concession [*despite what condition?*]	(al)though, even though	Charlie stayed there *even though he became bored.*

Adverb Clause Telling—	Introduced by Subordinating Conjunction—	Example
Result [*that what resulted?*]	that	They arrived so late *that no seats were left.*
Comparison [*to what degree?*]	as, than	She is taller *than I [am].*

For variety, emphasis, or clarity of sequence, you can shift most adverb clauses to the beginning of the sentence:

> *Wherever the trail led,* we followed it.
> *If you forget your raincoat,* you will be drenched.

Usually, a comma follows an adverb clause that begins a sentence.

A noun clause is used as a noun. It is introduced and connected to the independent clause by the relative pronoun *who(ever), which(ever),* or *what(ever),* or by *that, when, where, why, how,* or *whether.* The noun clause actually serves as part of the independent clause, such as subject or direct object:

> *What they had done* amazed everyone. [subject]
> No one believed *that Rollo had quit.* [direct object]
> She gave *whoever passed by* a brochure. [indirect object]
> She gave a brochure to *whoever passed by.* [object of preposition]
> *What we want to know* [subject] is *why you did it.* [subject complement]

> *Note:* As with adjective clauses, you may sometimes omit *that* (I understand ~~that~~ *you need help*), but in formal writing it is usually better to keep it. See 130C, page 29.

125C. Clauses in the Kinds of Sentences. As you learned in section 103B, sentences can be classified according to their structure (the number and kind[s] of clauses they have) as **simple, compound, complex,** or **compound-complex.** See page 2 for explanation and examples.

For resources to help you master this section's topics, log in to www.mywritinglab.com and select The Parts of Speech, Phrases and Clauses from the list of subtopics.

126–127. Agreement

In standard-English sentences, subject and verb must have matching forms; so must pronouns and their antecedents. This matching is called **agreement.** (See 402, page 52, for a definition of *standard English.*)

126. Subject–Verb Agreement. Every verb must agree with its subject in **person** and **number.**

126A. Agreement in Person. (*Person* is defined in 116, page 9.) Remember that third person singular verbs take an *-s* ending in the present tense and use *has* in the present perfect: She *walks* (or *has* walked), Joe *walks,* the dog *walks.*

> **Wrong (nonstandard):** Mae *sing* off key.
> **Right:** Mae **sings** off key.

There are no endings for other persons (except with *be*):

> I *walk,* we *walk* (or *have walked*) [first person]; you *walk* [second person]; they *walk,* the Smiths *walk,* the dogs *walk* [third person plural].

The verb *be* has different forms for each person:

Person	Singular	Plural
First	I am [*past,* was]	we are [*past,* were]
Second	you are [*past,* were]	you are [*past,* were]
Third	he/she/it is [*past,* was]	they are [*past,* were]

> **Wrong (nonstandard):** You *is* late. You *be* late. You *been* late. You *has been* late.
> **Right:** You **are** late. You **have been** late.

> *Note:* When two or more subjects in different persons are joined by *or,* the verb agrees with the subject nearer to it: Either *she* or *I am* going. In a dependent clause with *who* or *that* as subject, the verb agrees with the antecedent of *who* or *that:* It is *I* who *am* right. [Antecedent of *who* is *I.*]

126B. Agreement in Number. Singular number refers to one thing, and **plural** number refers to more than one. Singular subjects must take singular verbs; plural subjects must take plural verbs. As you just learned in 126A, the third person singular, present tense, needs an *-s* ending, and the verb *be* has irregular forms:

> **Wrong (nonstandard):** My *friend like* tacos, but *he don't* [do not] like burgers.
> **Right:** My *friend likes* tacos, but *he doesn't* [does not] like burgers.

> **Wrong (nonstandard):** Only one rock *concert have* been scheduled here.
> **Right:** Only one rock *concert has* been scheduled here.

> **Wrong (nonstandard):** *Was* all the *planes* delayed?
> **Right:** **Were** all the *planes* delayed?

A whole clause or phrase used as subject is singular—

> What their plans are **has** not been made known.
> Knowing when and how to respond **takes** years of experience.

—unless the sense is clearly plural:

> What once were their plans **are** no longer feasible.

21

126C. Intervening Word Groups. Make subject and verb agree regardless of phrases or clauses between them:

> **Phrase:** Their *performance* on all tests **is** impressive.
> **Clause:** *Cars* that failed a safety test **were** junked.
> An *employee* who accepts bribes, gratuities, or other favors from clients, even clients who are unaware of our rules, **is** subject to dismissal.

Parenthetical phrases introduced by (*together*) *with, like, as well as, including, in addition to,* and the like do not affect the number of the actual subject:

> The *burger,* as well as the fries, **is** laden with fat.
> *Aaron,* in addition to the twins, **has** brown eyes.

126D. Compound Subjects

Joined by *and*: Use a plural verb:

> A *rake* and a *shovel* **are** all I need.
> **Have** *Jennings* and *Greenly* arrived yet?

However, if both subjects refer to the same single person or thing, use a singular verb:

> Her *mentor and friend* **was** at her side during the ordeal. [One person is both mentor and friend.]
> *Macaroni and cheese* **is** on the menu. [one dish]

Use a singular verb when *each, every,* or *many a* precedes the subjects:

> *Every dog and cat* **is** tested for rabies.
> *Many a dog and cat* **is** wandering hungry tonight.

> **Note:** When *each follows* the subject, use a plural verb: The cat and the dog *each* **have** had their rabies shots.

Joined by *or* or *nor*: Make the verb agree with the nearer subject:

> *Spinach* or *kale* **was** added to the soup.
> *Peas* or *carrots* **were** added to the soup.
> *Spinach* or *peas* **were** added to the soup.
> *Peas* or *spinach* **was** added to the soup.

126E. Subjects accompanied by *not, and not, but not,* or *not only*. Make the verb agree with the subject *outside* the part containing *not*:

> Better *salaries,* [and] not a new building, **are** what we need.
> Not only better salaries but a new *building* **is** what we need.

126F. Indefinite Pronouns. Use a singular verb when the subject is a singular indefinite pronoun, such as *one, each, either, neither, everyone, everybody, anyone, anybody, someone, somebody, no one,* or *nobody.* Do not be misled by intervening phrases or clauses:

> *Each* of the blouses in the shipments **has** a tiny defect.
> *Everyone* who has ever seen any of her plays **is** calling this her best.

After *all, any, most, none, some,* or *such,* use either a singular or a plural verb, depending on whether the pronoun refers to something singular or plural:

> The milk was left in the sun; *all* of it **has** turned sour.
> The guests became bored; *all* **have** left.
> *Such* **were** the joys of youth. *Such* **is** the way of the world.

126G. Collective Nouns. In U.S. usage, use a singular verb when thinking of the group as a unit:

> The *audience* **was** the largest this season.

Use a plural verb when thinking of the group members as individuals:

> The *audience* **were** leaving, one or two at a time.

126H. Linking Verbs. Make a linking verb agree with its subject, not with its subject complement:

> His *problem* **was** wild pitches. Wild *pitches* **were** his problem.

126I. Singular Nouns in Plural Form. Such nouns as *measles, mumps, hives* (diseases); *mathematics, economics* (subjects of study); *billiards;* and *news* are singular. So is *United States* (one nation). Use a singular verb:

> *Mathematics* **is** not so difficult as many think.
> *Mumps* **leaves** some children with impaired hearing.
> The *United States* **has** a four-thousand-mile border with Canada.

Such nouns as *statistics, tactics, athletics,* and *ethics* are singular when they mean a single area of study or endeavor, but plural otherwise:

> *Statistics* **is** my major. New *statistics* **show** a drop in crime.
> *Athletics* **is** a big business today. *Athletics* **are** hard for him.

Use a plural verb with two-part things such as *trousers, pants, pliers, scissors, tweezers:*

> The *tweezers* **are** not useful here; perhaps the *pliers* **are**.

126J. *There, It,* and Inverted Order

There or *it* is sometimes an **expletive**; that is, a word that allows the real subject to follow the verb.

The expletive *there* is never the subject. In sentences beginning with *there is (was)* or *there are (were),* look *after* the verb for the subject, and make the verb agree with that subject:

> **Wrong:** There's two *taxis* at the curb. [Two *taxis is* . . .]
> There's a *taxi* and a *bus* at the curb. [A *taxi* and a *bus is.* . .]
> **Right:** There **is** a *taxi* at the curb. [A *taxi* **is** at the curb.]
> There **are** two *taxis* at the curb. [Two *taxis* **are** at the curb.] There **are** a *taxi* and a *bus* at the curb. [A *taxi* and a *bus* **are** . . .]

Wrong: Was there other *problems?*
*Right: **Was*** there another *problem?* ***Were*** there other *problems?*

The expletive *it*, on the other hand, is always singular:

*It **was*** my computer that malfunctioned.
*It **was*** our computers that malfunctioned.
Was *it* our computers that malfunctioned?

Inverted word order does not change subject–verb agreement:

Left on his shopping list ***were*** *beans, soup,* and *juice.* [*Beans, soup,* and *juice **were** . . .*]
Affixed to all the bulletin boards ***was*** *a list* of finalists. [A *list* of finalists ***was** . . .*]

126K. Literary Titles and Words Considered as Words are always singular:

Poe's *Tales of the Grotesque **was*** published in 1840.
*Zeroes **is*** spelled with either *-oes* or *-os.*

126L. Sums of Money and Measurements. When considering a sum as a single unit or total, use a singular verb:

*Sixty thousand dollars **is*** still owed on the mortgage.
*Fifteen hundred meters **is*** my longest race.

When considering individual dollars, gallons, miles, and so on, use a plural verb:

Old silver *dollars **are*** on display at the mint.
Those long, weary *miles **take*** a toll on my feet.

In an arithmetic problem, use either:

*Six and four **is [makes]*** ten. *Six and four **are [make]*** ten.

> *Note: The number* takes a singular verb; *a number,* plural: *The number* of crimes ***is*** down. *A number* of crimes ***are*** unsolved.

126M. Relative Pronouns. Use a singular verb if the antecedent of *who, which,* or *that* is singular; use a plural verb if the antecedent is plural:

This is the *dorm that **has*** air conditioning.
These are the *dorms that **have*** air conditioning.
This is the only *one* of the dorms *that **has*** air conditioning. [Only one has air conditioning; antecedent of *that* is *one.*]
This is one of several *dorms that **have*** air conditioning. [Several dorms have air conditioning; antecedent of *that* is *dorms.*]

127. Pronoun–Antecedent Agreement. Every pronoun must agree with its antecedent in person and number.

127A. Illogical Shifts to *You*. Avoid them:

Wrong: Students like English 302 because it exposes *you* to classic films. *I* like English 302 because it exposes *you* to classic films.

Right: Students like English 302 because it exposes ***them*** to classic films. *I* like English 302 because it exposes ***me*** to classic films.

127B. Singular Pronouns. Generally, use a singular pronoun when referring to antecedents such as *person, woman, man, one, anyone, anybody, someone, somebody, each, either, neither, everyone, everybody:*

Neither of the companies would recall ***its*** product.
Will each *woman* in the sorority pledge ***her*** loyalty?
Everyone on the football team played ***his*** best.
A *person* should know what ***he*** wants in life. [or *what **she** wants in life*]

For a mixed group of men and women, should you use *they, their, them* with a singular pronoun (*everyone* lost *their* money)? Do your best to avoid such constructions, but for help on this important, thorny problem, see 121A, page 16.

127C. Antecedents Joined by *and, or,* or *nor.* Follow the same principles as for subject–verb agreement (see 126D, page 22).

With antecedents joined by *and,* use a plural pronoun:

New York State and *New England* are noted for ***their*** fall foliage.

With antecedents joined by *or* or *nor,* make the pronoun agree with the nearer antecedent:

Visit *New York State* or *New England* for ***its*** fall foliage.
Visit *New York* or other northeastern *states* for ***their*** fall foliage.

127D. Collective Nouns. Follow the same principle as for subject–verb agreement (see 126G, page 22); let the sense of the noun determine the number of the pronoun:

The *staff* is meeting on ***its*** lunch hour.
The *staff* are taking ***their*** vacations at separate times.

127E. Demonstrative Pronouns Used as Adjectives. Make *this, that, these,* or *those* agree with the noun it modifies:

Wrong: I like *these kind* of fish. [*These* is plural; *kind,* singular.]
Right: I like ***this*** kind of fish. I like ***these*** kinds of fish.

127F. One of the. . . . After *one of the,* use a plural noun:

Wrong: This is *one of the* finest *novel* of the year.
Right: This is *one of the* finest *novel**s*** of the year.

*For resources to help you master this section's topics, log in to www.mywritinglab.com and select Subject-Verb Agreement **and** Pronoun-Antecedent Agreement from the list of subtopics.*

128–130. Clear, Effective Sentences

Effective sentences are more than just correct. Good writers edit each sentence to ensure clarity, precision, smoothness, economy, originality, and harmony with the rest of the paragraph.

128. Creating Effective Sentences

128A. Vary Your Sentences. Sentences that plod dully along one after another, unvaried in length or structure, bore your readers and sap their attention. One short, simple sentence can be forceful: *The money was gone.* But a string of short sentences usually sounds choppy and immature:

> The aid workers were all volunteers. They flew to earthquake-stricken Haiti. They fed the starving. They nursed the sick.

Strings of clauses joined by *and* or *and so* are little better:

> The aid workers were all volunteers, and they flew to earthquake-stricken Haiti, and they fed the starving and they nursed the sick.

(A good writer might say *The aid workers, all volunteers, flew to earthquake-stricken Haiti, where they fed the starving and nursed the sick.*)

At the other extreme, a series of long, complex sentences can also stupefy. Like a good baseball pitcher, vary what you serve up. This section (128) shows you how to do so.

Vary your sentence beginnings where appropriate. You need not always start with the subject; try moving a modifying word, phrase, or clause to the beginning, or shift word order for emphasis:

> *To reach the summit,* the climbers had to start before dawn.
> *Terrified, freezing, and weak with hunger,* the refugees plodded on.
> *This kind of music* the audience had never heard before.

Caution: Do not vary just for variety's sake; you may weaken your paper, for example, by switching from active voice to passive merely for variety or by moving a modifier to an unnatural position. Judging when and how to vary becomes easier with wider experience in reading.

128B. Use Coordination. You can join related simple sentences with a coordinating conjunction (preceded by a comma) to form a compound sentence:

> **Choppy (short, simple sentences):** The painting was twelve inches square. It was valued at a million dollars.
> **Better (compound sentence):** The painting was twelve inches square, **yet** it was valued at a million dollars. [The conjunction *yet* emphasizes the contrast between the size and the value.]

> **Choppy:** Professor Budway retired. His health had worsened.
> **Better:** Professor Budway retired, **for** his health had worsened. [The conjunction *for* clarifies that the second fact caused the first.]

> **Choppy:** The Miami plane left late. The Orlando plane's crew never showed up.
> **Better:** The Miami plane left late, **and** the Orlando plane's crew never showed up. [The *and,* though it has little effect on meaning, shows that the two ideas are related and makes a smoother-reading sentence.]

Avoid overuse of coordination, especially with *and* or *so.*

See 107A, page 4, for more on coordinating conjunctions.

128C. Use Compounding. Combine simple sentences that have the same subjects, verbs, or other parts so that you have only one sentence, with a compound part:

> **Weak:** The Republicans are supporting the bill. The Democrats are also supporting it.
> **Stronger (compound subject): [Both]** the *Republicans* **and** the *Democrats* are supporting the bill.

> **Weak:** Senator Lynch will sponsor the bill. She will also campaign for it.
> **Stronger (compound verb):** Senator Lynch will *[both]* sponsor **and** campaign for the bill.

> **Weak:** The bill raises farm subsidies. It also cuts taxes.
> **Stronger (compound complete predicate):** The bill *raises farm subsidies* **and** *cuts taxes.* OR The bill **not only** *raises farm subsidies* **but also** *cuts taxes.*

128D. Use Subordination. In combining simple sentences, you can emphasize one idea by subordinating the other (reducing it to a dependent clause). Often, subordinating is the clearest way to show how two ideas are related. It is one of the most important skills in good sentence writing. You may subordinate with (1) adjective clauses, (2) adverb clauses, or (3) noun clauses (see 125B, page 20, for explanation of these terms).

Adjective clauses (beginning with *who* [*whose, whom*], *which, that, when,* or *where*) let you show which of two ideas you consider more important. Put the *more* important idea into the independent clause, the *less* important one into the adjective clause:

> **Weak:** Saturn is the sixth planet from the sun. It has a unique set of rings.
> **Weak:** Saturn is the sixth planet from the sun, and it has a unique set of rings.

Strengthened by adjective-clause subordination:

> Saturn, **which** *is the sixth planet from the sun,* has a unique set of rings. [Sentence stresses the rings—the independent clause.]
> Saturn, **which** *has a unique set of rings,* is the sixth planet from the sun. [Sentence stresses the planet's order from the sun—the independent clause.]

Adverb clauses (beginning with *when, if, because, although* . . .—see 125B, page 20, for full list) let you show that two ideas are related by time, cause, condition, and the like:

> **Weak:** The film grew boring. We left the theater early.

Strengthened by adverb-clause subordination:

> **When** *the film grew boring,* we left the theater early.
> [*When* stresses the time relation between the two facts.]
> We left the theater early **because** *the film had grown boring.* [*Because* stresses the causal relation between the two facts.]

Noun clauses (beginning with *who, that, what, whatever* . . .—see 125B, page 20, for full list) provide smoothness and conciseness:

> **Weak:** Mayor Zilch had embezzled public funds. The voters never knew this.
> **Weak:** Some children are underachievers. Karp's research discovered the reasons for this problem.

Strengthened by noun-clause subordination:

> The voters never knew **that** *Mayor Zilch had embezzled public funds.*
> Karp's research discovered **why** *some children are under-achievers.*

With subordination, compounding, and coordination, you can smoothly integrate three or even more ideas:

> **Weak:** Walt Disney created a new genre of film. He produced the first feature-length color cartoon, *Snow White.* The film transformed the well-known fairy tale. It blended comedy and drama. It also had original songs.
> **Subordinated and coordinated:** Walt Disney created a new genre of film **when** he produced the first feature-length color cartoon, *Snow White,* **which** transformed the well-known fairy tale into a blend of comedy, drama, **and** original songs.

Subordination can be even more effective when combined with **reduction,** explained in 128E.

Caution: Do not overdo subordination; four or five clauses inexpertly combined in a sentence can bewilder readers. And never subordinate your main idea—the one you would mention if you could mention only one. See 128G.

128E. Use Reduction. Whenever possible, eliminate needless words by reducing clauses to phrases and phrases to single words:

> **Wordy (clause):** *Because she was discouraged about writing stories,* Erika decided to try nonfiction.
> **Tighter (phrase):** *Discouraged about writing stories,* Erika decided to try nonfiction.

> **Wordy (clause):** The person *who is holding the pistol* is the starter.
> **Tighter (phrase):** The person *holding the pistol* is the starter.

> **Wordy (phrase):** She is a child *possessed of talent.*
> **Tighter (word):** She is a *talented* child.

Here is the last example from 128D, further tightened by reduction:

> Walt Disney created a new genre of film when he produced the first feature-length color cartoon, *Snow White,*

transforming the well-known fairy tale by *blending* comedy, drama, and original songs.

For more on cutting needless words, see 401A, page 50.

128F. Use Parallel Structure (the same grammatical form for each item in a series), wherever appropriate, in coordinating or comparing:

> **Wrong—not parallel:** They tried flattering [gerund] and to cajole [infinitive] him.
> **Right:** They tried flattering and cajoling him.
> **Right:** They tried to flatter and [to] cajole him.

> **Wrong:** Football trainers reminded their players about helmet-to-helmet *hits* [noun], not *to get dehydrated* [infinitive], and *they need to do stretching exercises* [clause].
> **Right:** Football trainers reminded their players about helmet-to-helmet *hits* [noun], *dehydration* [noun], and stretching *exercises* [noun].

> **Wrong:** Job seekers should *consult* the want ads [verb], their friends [no verb], or *look* online [verb].
> **Right:** Job seekers should *consult* the want ads [verb], *ask* their friends [verb], or *look* online [verb].
> **Right:** Job seekers should consult the *want ads* [noun], their *friends* [noun], or online *sources* [noun].

> **Wrong:** Their alienation might have been caused by an unfortunate *event* [noun], *they* just *lost* interest [clause], a marriage *issue* [noun], or *we* just *do* not *know* why [clause].
> **Right:** Their alienation might have been caused by an unfortunate *event* [noun], a *loss* of interest [noun], a marriage *issue* [noun], or *something* unknown to us [pronoun].

> *Note:* Jotting each series item in a column can help you see whether the items are parallel and correct them if not.

Use parallelism to emphasize likeness or contrast:

> **Wrong:** Ethanol has been hailed by some environmentalists who say it reduces pollution, but other environmentalists have claimed that pollution is increased by it. [mixes active and passive]
> **Right:** Some environmentalists claim that ethanol pollutes less; others, that it pollutes more.

Use parallelism in comparisons (with *as* or *than*):

> **Wrong:** The sculpture was **more** odd [adjective] **than** it impressed us [clause].
> **Right:** The sculpture was **more** odd [adjective] **than** impressive [adjective].

Use parallelism with correlative conjunctions (*both . . . and; not only . . . but also; [n]either . . . [n]or*). What directly follows the second part of the conjunction should be parallel to what follows the first:

> **Wrong:** Our tour **not only** visited [verb] Madrid **but also** Barcelona [noun].
> **Right:** Our tour visited **not only** Madrid [noun] **but also** Barcelona [noun].

Wrong: Last season ***not only*** did the Colts defeat the Bears ***but also*** the Vikings. [Misplacement of *not only . . . but also* makes it unclear who defeated whom.]

Right: Last season the Colts defeated ***not only*** the Bears ***but also*** the Vikings. [Colts won two.]

Right: Last season ***not only*** the Colts ***but also*** the Vikings defeated the Bears. [Bears lost two.]

Be sure your items are parallel logically as well as grammatically:

Illogical: The city has *three museums, a concert hall, an opera house,* and *a high crime rate.* [The crime rate does not belong with the other items, which are cultural attractions. Avoid such illogic, unless you intend irony.]

Other examples of parallel structure:

Is it better *to die with honor* than *to live in shame?*
She neither *sought* nor *desired* the nomination.
Brilliant in conception, revolutionary in structure, and *elegant in orchestration,* her new symphony was universally praised.

Marlowe was the only one of the university wits whose talent Shakespeare might have seriously envied, whose aesthetic judgment he might have feared, whose admiration he might have earnestly wanted to win, and whose achievements he certainly attempted to equal and outdo.
—Stephen Greenblatt

128G. Position Main Ideas Prominently

Do not bury your main point in the middle of your sentence, in a phrase or dependent clause:

Poor—intended main idea (*winning first prize*) **lost in midsentence,** in a dependent clause: Dwight's essay on creating inner-city jobs, *which won first prize,* competed agaist fifty others.

For proper emphasis, put your main idea at the beginning or sometimes at the end (as a climax):

Emphatic—main point up front: Dwight *won first prize* over fifty others for his essay on creating inner-city jobs.

Emphatic and climactic—main point at end: Competing against fifty others with his essay on creating inner-city jobs, Dwight *won first prize.*

Get to the point. Do not hide your real subject by opening your sentence with clutter:

Cluttered: In the final analysis, it is important to note that the initial reason that the effects I have mentioned took place is the *defaulting* by homeowners on subprime mortgages.

Clear and direct: In short, it was homeowners' *defaulting* on subprime mortgages that caused the chain of events described above.

See 401A, page 50, for more on removing clutter.

129. Overcoming Faulty Sentence Structure

Fragments, comma splices, and **fused sentences** are the most common, and often the most obvious, of major lapses in sentence structure. Make it a priority to rid your papers

of these faults. Review sections 124–125, on phrases and clauses (pages 19–21), if necessary.

129A. Fragments. A fragment is a piece of a sentence mistakenly written as a full sentence. It may be

A phrase: In the woods. Sleeping in the woods.

A dependent clause, sometimes with part of another clause: When they slept in the woods. That slept in the woods. The campers, who slept in the woods.

Just a verbless string of words: The woods dark and deep. Three miles farther away, beyond the forest.

Correct every fragment by either

Attaching it to an independent clause: *Sleeping in the woods,* the campers did not hear the news. The campers did not hear the news *because they were sleeping in the woods.* The campers, *who were sleeping in the woods,* did not hear the news.

Or making the fragment into a full sentence: They slept *in the woods.* Camp was *three miles farther away, beyond the forest.*

In the examples below, the fragments and their correct revisions are in *italics.*

Wrong: People may have trouble sleeping at night. *Because they drink alcohol or caffeinated beverages too close to bedtime.*

Right: People may have trouble sleeping at night *because they drink alcohol or caffeinated beverages too close to bedtime.* [fragment attached to independent clause]

Wrong: Clogging of leg arteries usually goes hand in hand with blocking of arteries leading to the heart and brain. *Which increases the risk of heart attack or stroke.*

Right: Clogging of leg arteries usually goes hand in hand with blocking of arteries leading to the heart and brain, *which increases the risk of heart attack or stroke.* [fragment attached to independent clause]

Wrong: A woman whom everyone admires.

Right: Bella Isola is a woman whom everyone admires. [fragment rewritten as a full sentence]

Wrong: Her mother a maid in a rich family's house, and her father a sailor on an oil tanker.

Right: Her mother was *a maid in a rich family's house, and her father* was *a sailor on an oil tanker.* [verbs added to make a sentence]

Wrong: Security was particularly tight at Kennedy Airport. *Being a main entry point for smugglers.*
OR *It being a main entry point for smugglers.*
OR *A main entry point for smugglers.*

Right: Security was particularly tight at Kennedy Airport, *a main entry point for smugglers.* [fragment attached as appositive]

129B. Comma Splices and Fused Sentences. A comma splice is the mistaken joining of independent clauses with just a comma rather than a conjunction or semicolon:

Wrong: Running relieves stress, it can prolong life. OR Running relieves stress, therefore it can prolong life.

Wrong: Scientists report progress in channeling brain waves to run mechanical devices, this could someday help paralyzed people walk.

A **fused sentence** is the mistaken joining of independent clauses with no punctuation or conjunction at all:

Wrong: Running relieves stress it can prolong life.
Wrong: Scientists report progress in channeling brain waves to run mechanical devices this could someday help paralyzed people walk.

Correct splices and fusings (both sometimes called **run-ons**) in one of the following four ways; choose the way that best fits your purpose and your paragraph:

Separate the clauses into two sentences:

Right: Running relieves stress. It can prolong life.

This is the simplest but usually not the best way, for too many short sentences make your writing sound choppy and immature (see 128A, page 24). Moreover, you fail to specify a relation between the ideas in the clauses.

Join the clauses with a coordinating conjunction:

Right: Running relieves stress, *and* it can prolong life.

Coordinating is often better than writing separate sentences. But do not overuse coordinating either; the conjunction *and,* especially, may not clarify the relation between your ideas. (See 128B, page 24.)

Join the clauses with a semicolon:

Right: Running relieves stress; it can prolong life.
Right: Running relieves stress; thus it can prolong life.

A semicolon can give your writing a formal tone; it is often effective in balanced sentences, such as *Yesterday was dreadful; today is delightful.* (See 210A, B, page 36.)

Join the clauses by making one of them a dependent (subordinate) clause. Join them with a subordinating conjunction, such as *because, if, when, since, after, although,* and *unless,* or with a relative pronoun: *who(m), which, that.* (See 128D pages 24–25.) Subordinating is often the best way to eliminate splices and fusings, because a subordinating conjunction or relative pronoun shows the precise relation between ideas:

Right: Running, *which* relieves stress, can prolong life.
Right: Running can prolong life, *because* it relieves stress.

Here are more corrected comma splices (fused sentences are corrected the same way):

Wrong: Scientists report progress in channeling brain waves to run mechanical devices, this could someday help paralyzed people walk.
Right: Scientists report progress in channeling brain waves to run mechanical devices; such a breakthrough could someday help paralyzed people walk. [clauses joined by semicolon]

Wrong: Cole's study (2009) concluded that pupils with more stable home environments had higher reading scores, this finding corroborated Lynch's 2002 findings.
Right: . . . higher reading scores, a finding that corroborated Lynch's 2002 findings. [last clause subordinated]
Right: . . . higher reading scores. This finding corroborated Lynch's 2002 findings. [last clause made separate sentence]

130. Ensuring Clarity and Smoothness Clarity is a writer's first obligation. If you are not clear, you are not communicating. Clear sentences, moreover, are usually smoother.

If you blend your common sense with what you have learned about grammar and sentence structure, your sentences will ring clear and true, free of the faults described below and elsewhere in *English Simplified.* (Clarity in using pronouns is treated in 123; in using punctuation, 201F, 202A, 211E, 212A, and 226D; in word choice, 401A and 404; in writing paragraphs, 503.)

130A. Needless Separation of Related Sentence Parts

Do not needlessly separate subject and verb, or verb and completer:

Awkward: I, having forgotten to fill the gasoline tank or even recharge my cell phone, *found* myself marooned on a deserted road.
Smooth: Having forgotten to fill the gasoline tank or even recharge my cell phone, *I found* myself marooned on a deserted road.

Awkward: They *bought,* by emptying their bank accounts and cashing in their bonds, a large *house.*
Smooth: By emptying their bank accounts and cashing in their bonds, they *bought* a large *house.*

Avoid awkward splitting of infinitives. The two parts of an infinitive belong together; avoid putting words between them (unless your resulting sentence would be unclear or sound odd):

Wrong: He wanted *to* at least once a week *call* her.
Right: He wanted *to call* her at least once a week.

It is quite all right, however, to place an appropriate adverb within the infinitive: They decided *to quickly replace* the dog that had died.

Avoid ending a sentence with a preposition in formal writing (unless your resulting sentence would sound awkward or stilted):

Informal: This is the house that Melville lived *in.*
Formal: This is the house *in which* Melville lived.

Note: Some verbs contain a *particle*—a word that looks like a preposition but is actually part of the meaning of the verb—e.g., *call up, find out, give up, blow up* (explode), *put up with.* It is perfectly all right—sometimes necessary—to end a formal sentence with a particle: He had forgotten her telephone number and had to *look* it *up.* A verb + particle is sometimes called a *phrasal verb.*

130B. Misplaced or Dangling Modifiers A modifying word, phrase, or clause in the wrong place can make your sentence unclear, confusing, or unintentionally funny. (An old joke: "Last night I chased an elephant in my pajamas. Why it was wearing my pajamas I'll never know!")

Misplaced Modifiers

Place each modifier (word, phrase, or clause) as close as possible to the word it modifies:

Adverb:

> *Wrong:* It was sad that the cousins *almost* **lost** all their savings in the swindle. [*Almost lost* means that they came close to losing but lost nothing.]
> *Right:* It was sad that the cousins lost *almost* **all** their savings in the swindle.

This same caution applies with *only, nearly, scarcely, hardly, just,* and *even: Only* **Sean** sampled the pizza, Sean *only* **sampled** the pizza, and Sean sampled *only* the **pizza** all have different meanings.

Phrase:

> *Wrong:* The Brewsters watched the President announce that he would raise **taxes** *on television.* [Will there be a tax on television?]
> *Right:* The Brewsters watched the President **announce** *on television* that he would raise taxes.

> *Wrong* [a letter to the president of the Civic League]: *As president of the Civic League,* **I** insist that you urge the League to encourage voter registration.
> *Right:* I insist that **you,** *as president of the Civic League,* urge the League to encourage voter registration.

> *Wrong: Nearing collapse, having been idle for almost forty years,* **Charles and Cathy Wright** bought the mill in 1992 and began restoration. [Were the Wrights near collapse and long idle?]
> *Right:* In 1992 Charles and Cathy Wright bought the **mill,** *nearing collapse after lying idle for forty years,* and began restoration.

> *Note:* You may separate a phrase from the word it modifies if there is no possibility of a misreading: Tiffany left the party shortly after midnight, *filled with curiosity about the man she had just met.* [The italicized phrase clearly refers only to *Tiffany.*]

Clause:

> *Wrong:* The taxi driver from the airport was surprised to learn that **I** was American, *as were the vendors in the fruit markets.* [Were the vendors American?]
> *Right:* The taxi **driver** from the airport, *as well as the vendors in the fruit markets,* was surprised to learn that I was American.

> *Wrong:* For their short feeding trips, we tape waterproof tags to the birds' **backs**, *which are then removed and reused.* [Are the backs removed and reused?]
> *Right:* For their short feeding trips, we tape to the birds' backs waterproof **tags**, *which are then removed and reused.*

Avoid "squinting" modifiers. A squinter comes between two words so that the reader cannot tell to which word it refers:

> *Wrong:* He **promised** *immediately* to **repay** the money. [This can have either of the two meanings below.]
> *Right:* He *immediately* **promised** to repay the money.
> *Right:* He promised to **repay** the money *immediately.*

> *Wrong:* A coalition of groups concerned about the state-wide **rise** in home foreclosures *last month* **urged** the governor to create a $100 million dollar fund to address the issue. [Which happened last month—the rise or the urging?]
> *Right: Last month* a coalition of groups **urged** . . .
> *Right (other meaning):* A coalition of groups concerned about *last month's* **rise** in home foreclosures . . .

Be especially careful with negatives, with possessives, and before *and*:

> *Wrong:* It was **not** her first arrest, *as she had told the lawyer.* [Had she told the lawyer that it *was* her first arrest, or that it *was not*?]
> *Right: As she had told the lawyer,* it was **not** her first arrest.
> *Right (other meaning):* It was **not** her first arrest, *though she had told the lawyer it was.*

> *Wrong (printed on a medication box):* Attention pharmacist—dispense contents with the *enclosed* **patient's** instructions for use. [Was the patient enclosed in the box?]
> *Right:* Attention pharmacist—dispense contents with the *enclosed* **instructions** for patient's use.

> *Wrong:* The school office was crowded with *late* **students** and **teachers.** [Were only the students late, or both teachers and students?]
> *Right:* The school office was crowded with teachers and *late* **students.** [Only the students were late.]
> *Right (other meaning):* The school office was crowded with **students** and **teachers,** all *late.*

Dangling Modifiers

A modifying phrase is said to dangle when it cannot logically modify any word in the sentence: *Walking down the stairs,* an exit **sign** caught Pat's eye. The structure of this sentence (ridiculously) has the sign walking down the stairs, since *sign* is the nearest noun to the phrase. The sentence should read *Walking down the stairs,* **Pat** caught sight of an exit sign.

Correct a dangler in any of the ways shown below.

Dangling participle:

> *Wrong: Painting its siding every three years,* the house's **appearance** remained immaculate. [Who did the painting? The nearest noun to the phrase should name the person who did.]
> *Right: Painting the house's siding every three years,* the **Ramirezes** kept its appearance immaculate. [name of painters, the *Ramirezes,* put nearest to phrase]

Right: The house retained its immaculate appearance *because the* **Ramirezes painted** *its siding every three years.* [phrase expanded into clause naming painters]

Note: Possessives do not count as the "nearest noun":

Wrong: *Painting its siding every three years*, the Ramirezes' **house** kept its appearance immaculate.

Right: See examples above this note.

Dangling gerund:

Wrong: *After completing a pretrial rehabilitation program*, **charges** against Jones were dropped. [Did the charges complete the program?]

Right: *After completing a pretrial rehabilitation program*, **Jones** had the charges against him dropped.

Right: *After* **Jones completed** *a pretrial rehabilitation program*, charges against him were dropped.

Dangling infinitive:

Wrong: *To appreciate the play*, a good **seat** is needed. [Who is appreciating the play? Not the seat.]

Wrong: *To appreciate the play*, the **box office** needs to give you a good seat. [Is the box office appreciating the play?]

Right: *To appreciate the play*, **you** need a good seat.

Right: *To appreciate the play*, get a good seat. [*You* is the understood subject of *get*.]

Dangling elliptical clause.
An elliptical clause is one from which the subject and all or part of the verb have been dropped as understood:

Full clause: When I was skiing in Utah

Elliptical clause: When skiing in Utah

Use an elliptical clause only when its (understood) subject is the *same* as the subject of the following clause: When I̶ w̶a̶s̶ skiing in Utah, **I** made a lifelong friend. (*I* is the subject of both clauses.)

Wrong: While on the wrestling team, Leo's **dog** came along to practices. [Was the dog on the team?]

Right: While on the wrestling team, **Leo** took his dog along to practices. [subject of second clause made same as understood subject of elliptical clause]

Right: While **Leo was** on the wrestling team, **he** took his dog along to practices. [subject and verb of elliptical clause restored]

130C. Omission of Needed Words

Incomplete or illogical comparisons

Wrong: The test was *so* easy.

Right: The test was *so* easy *that everyone passed.*

Wrong: Matthew visits his *father more than* his *sister.* [Who visits whom?]

Right: Matthew visits his father *more than he visits his sister.*

Right (other meaning): Matthew visits his father *more than his sister does.*

Wrong: His hair was shaggier *than* an ape. [Sentence compares *hair* with *ape*. Items compared must be of the same kind.]

Right: His hair was shaggier *than that of* an ape. [*That* stands for *hair;* sentence now compares hair with hair.]

Right: His hair was shaggier *than* an ape's [an ape's hair]. [Remember the apostrophe.]

Wrong: Mount McKinley rises higher *than* any peak in North America. [Since McKinley is included among North American peaks, you are saying that McKinley is higher than itself.]

Right: Mount McKinley rises higher *than* any *other* peak in North America.

Right: Mount McKinley is the highest peak in North America.

Omitted *that* Introducing a Clause

Keep *that* at the beginning of a clause if your sentence may mislead without it. For example, a reader starts your sentence: *The searchers found Maxwell* . . .

But your full sentence is: *The searchers found Maxwell had left the area* [a very different meaning]. By adding *that,* you become clear on first reading: The searchers found *that* Maxwell had left the area.

See 130E for more examples of omitted words.

130D. Illogical Shifts. You have already learned to avoid illogical shifts in person and number (Agreement: 126–127, pages 21–23) and in verb tense (118B, page 13). Avoid all illogical shifts in your focus within a sentence, such as from one subject or one verb form to another:

Wrong: As the *customers poured* through the doors, *bins* filled with bargains *could be seen*. [*Poured* is active voice; *could be seen*, passive. Also, subject shifts confusingly from *customers* to *bins*.]

Right: As the *customers poured* through the doors, *they could see* bins filled with bargains.

Wrong: Math scores *are creeping* up, but reading scores *have* not. [The omitted second verb must have the same form as the first verb (*creeping*), but *have not creeping* makes no sense.]

Right: Math scores *are creeping* up, but reading scores *are* not. [*are not creeping*]

Right: Math scores *have crept* up, but reading scores *have* not. [*have not crept*]

130E. Mixed or Confused Construction. Never lose control of a sentence. When finishing each sentence, keep in mind how you began it. All its parts must fit together both grammatically and logically.

Be sure that your subject, verb, and other sentence parts make sense together:

Wrong: The car's long-overdue *inspection cost* us $300 to have repaired. [The inspection did not cost $300 and need repairing.]

Right: At its long-overdue inspection, the *car cost* us $300 to have repaired.

Wrong: The police car *swerved the corner* on two wheels. [*Swerved* does not take an object.]

Right: The police car *swerved around the corner* on two wheels.

Wrong: Municipal Stadium was renamed *Hyundai Field,* a Korean auto *company.* [*Company* does not = *field.*]

Right: Municipal Stadium was renamed *Hyundai Field, for* a Korean auto *company.*

Avoid using an adverb clause as the subject of an action verb. A subject must tell *who* or *what,* not just *when, why,* or *where*:

Wrong: *Because the Democrats control the state legislature* [adverb clause telling *why*] gives them the power to appoint judges.

Right: The Democrats' *control* [noun as subject] of the state legislature gives them the power to appoint judges.

Right: Because the Democrats control the state legislature, *they* have the power to appoint judges. [*Because* clause is subordinated; *they* becomes subject of main clause.]

Wrong: *If he is found guilty* [adverb clause] means *that he will go to prison* [noun clause].

Right: A guilty *verdict* [noun] means *that he will go to prison* [noun clause].

Right (first clause subordinated): If he is found guilty, he will go to prison.

Do not mix indirect- and direct-question word order:

Wrong: She asked *when did they leave.* [direct-question word order in indirect question]

Right: She asked *when they had left.* [indirect question]

Right: She asked, "*When did they leave?*" [direct question]

For more on indirect questions, see 204A, page 34.

When equating two things, be sure both are grammatically and logically equal (=):

Wrong: Her favorite *pastime* was *at the movies.* [Pastime does not = place; a pastime is not a place.]

Right: Her favorite *pastime* was *going to the movies.* [Pastime = pastime.]

Wrong: Osteoporosis is *when* [or is *where*] a person's bones become soft. [*When* and *where* refer to time and place, but osteoporosis is a condition, not a time or place.]

Right: Osteoporosis [condition] is the *softening* [condition] of a person's bones. [Condition = condition.]

Wrong: At the arena, *sellouts of fifteen thousand,* common before the gambling scandals, *were* now only *three or four thousand.* [Sellouts (fifteen thousand) do not = three or four thousand.]

Right: *Crowds* that had commonly sold out the fifteen-thousand-seat arena before the gambling scandals now *shrank to* only *three or four thousand.* [Crowds = crowds.]

In sum, keep track of your overall structure—especially in a longer sentence:

Wrong: In 1947 the color *barrier* in baseball *was broken,* and the Brooklyn *Dodgers promoted* Jackie Robinson to the parent club. [Passive and active voices are mixed; the *and* makes event 2 seem to follow event 1, but in reality event 2 caused event 1.]

Right: In 1947 the Brooklyn *Dodgers broke* the color barrier in baseball *by promoting* Jackie Robinson to the parent club.

Wrong: Little did anyone think that the advent of Jackie Robinson would have *such a* revolutionary effect on the major leagues *since* the inception of league play in 1871. [*Such a* expresses degree, but *since* expresses time; the two do not make sense together.]

Right: Little did anyone think that the advent of Jackie Robinson would have *the most* revolutionary effect on the major leagues *since* the inception of league play in 1871. [*The most . . . since 1871* compares events of two times.]

For resources to help you master this section's topics, log in to www.mywritinglab.com and select Varying Sentence Structure, Consistent Verb Tense and Active Voice, Parallelism, Combining Sentences, Fragments, Run-Ons, Misplaced or Dangling Modifiers, and Sentence Structure from the list of subtopics.

Without punctuation, much of our writing would be hard to comprehend. Punctuation marks keep our writing clear by *separating* words or ideas, by *grouping* them, or by *emphasizing* them.

201–203. The Comma [,]

Misuse of the comma is the most common punctuation fault. To avoid comma calamities, follow the rules below—and work on developing a good ear for spoken pauses and stops; commas usually (though not always) match oral pauses.

201. Use a Comma to Set Off

201A. Independent (Main) Clauses. When two independent clauses are joined by *and, but, or, nor, for, yet,* or *so* (a coordinating conjunction), put a comma at the end of the first clause:

> The polls closed at 9 p.m., *and* the results soon came pouring in.
> The first election returns showed Senator Filch winning, *but* the vote soon began to shift against him.
> Filch may lose badly, *or* he may have a late winning surge.

However, do **not** use a comma

- Generally, if there is no full clause (subject + verb) after the conjunction:

  Wrong: They voted on the bill Monday, *and* adjourned Tuesday.

  Right: They voted on the bill Monday *and* adjourned Tuesday.

- *After* the conjunction:

  Wrong: They voted on the bill Monday *but,* it was defeated.

  Right: They voted on the bill Monday, *but* it was defeated.

- Between very short independent clauses:

  Right: She runs and he swims.

- Between independent clauses not joined by a coordinating conjunction (use a semicolon instead):

  Wrong: The alarm clock buzzed, Eva jumped out of bed. [This is a comma splice, a serious error. See 129B, page 26.]

  Right: The alarm clock buzzed; Eva jumped out of bed.

201B. Introductory Elements

An introductory adverb clause:

> *If you need help next week,* we will be glad to assist you.
> *When my parents retire from teaching,* they plan to move to Florida.

> **Note:** When the adverb clause *follows* the independent clause, you usually do not need a comma: My parents plan to move to Florida *when they retire from teaching.* (See 201F note, page 32, on *because* clauses.)

A long prepositional phrase or a series of prepositional phrases:

> *For the rest of the spring semester,* Marco dated Teresa.

Unless clarity or pacing demands one, you do not need a comma after one short introductory prepositional phrase:

> *In the spring* Marco dated Teresa.

A verbal phrase (infinitive, gerund, or participial):

> *To obtain financial aid,* you must complete a long application.
> *By applying early,* you can expect a fast response.
> *Swamped with last-minute applications,* the aid office fell behind.

An infinitive or gerund phrase used as the *subject* of a sentence is not an introductory element. Do not set it off:

> *To obtain financial aid* was her goal.
> *Submitting the application early* is a good idea.

An adverb or phrase applying to the whole following statement, not just to the verb:

> *Oddly,* the newlyweds went to Greenland on their honeymoon. [*Oddly* describes not how the newlyweds went but the writer's comment on the whole statement.]
> *Without a doubt,* they did not realize what they were doing.

(Such a construction is called a *sentence adverb* or *sentence modifier.* See *hopefully,* 402C, page 52.)

201C. Items in a Series. Use commas to separate words, phrases, or clauses in a series of three or more:

> ***Words:*** They considered *Hawaii, Cancun, Rio,* or *Jamaica* for their honeymoon.
> ***Phrases:*** The bikers roared *through the park, down the main street, and into the Capitol parking lot.*
> ***Clauses:*** *The stock market declined, interest rates fell,* and *real estate values tumbled.* Financial analysts wondered *why all this had occurred, whether the market would rebound,* and *what might happen in coming years.*

> **Note:** Some writers omit the comma before the final *and* or *or* in a series. Including this comma, however, ensures clarity.
> Use a comma before *etc.* at the end of a series: pork, beans, etc. (See *etc.,* 401A, page 50; 402C, page 52.)

Do **not** use a comma

- With only two items: She sought *peace* and *quiet.*
- If you repeat *and* or *or* between each two items: She sought *peace* and *quiet* and *solitude.*
- Before the first item or after the last:

  Wrong: She sought, *peace, quiet,* and *solitude.*

  Right: She sought *peace, quiet,* and *solitude.*

Wrong: Peace, quiet, and *solitude,* proved elusive.
Right: Peace, quiet, and *solitude* proved elusive.

201D. Coordinate Adjectives. In a series of two or more, use commas to separate adjectives of the same kind and importance (called *coordinate adjectives*). Think of the commas as substitutes for *and:* a cold *and* blustery *and* miserable day = a cold, blustery, miserable day [no comma follows the last adjective]:

> Hefty, expensive textbooks are not always the best.
> Too much fried, fatty, greasy food harms one's health.

Do not use commas between modifiers that are not coordinate (that is, the commas are not substituting for *and*):

- If a modifier describes the following adjective(s) rather than the noun: a *deep blue* car [*Deep* is describing *blue,* not *car.*]
- If the last adjective is considered part of the noun: a *tall pine* tree [*pine tree* is really one item; *tall* is modifying *pine tree*].
- If the adjectives are of different kinds; see 120D, page 15.

201E. Parenthetical Expressions. These are words or word groups that interrupt the flow of thought in a sentence but are not necessary to the sentence; they can be removed from the sentence without changing its essential meaning. Set such expressions off with a pair of commas, which act almost like parentheses:

> Elvira will be, *in my opinion,* the winner.
> Glenda, *on the other hand,* has a good chance.
> The race, *moreover,* is too long for Elvira.
> Sid is too shy, *to be frank.* [Notice the great difference in meaning from *Sid is too shy to be frank.*]

Some other common parenthetical expressions:

as a matter of fact	incidentally	by the way
to tell the truth	in the first place	of course

Within a clause, words such as *however, therefore,* and *nevertheless* (called *conjunctive adverbs*) are punctuated as parenthetical:

> One senator, *however,* remained unconvinced. The others, *nevertheless,* voted yes.

See 210B, page 36, for more on conjunctive adverbs.

> **Note:** You may choose not to set off *perhaps, likewise, at least, indeed, therefore, thus,* and certain similar expressions in sentences where you feel they do not interrupt your thought flow or where you want to emphasize them:
> **Right:** She was, *indeed,* a vivacious youngster.
> **Also right:** She was *indeed* a vivacious youngster.

201F. Nonessential (Nonrestrictive) Clauses, Phrases, and Appositives

Nonessential clauses. Put commas around clauses that are not essential to the meaning of the sentence (think of them as parenthetical expressions):

> My father's portrait, *which had hung in our hallway for years,* was sold at auction.
> It was painted by Aunt Letitia, *who had studied art in Paris.*

Explanation: Without the italicized clauses, the above sentences say

> My father's portrait was sold at auction.
> It was painted by Aunt Letitia.

Do we still know which painting was sold and who painted it? Yes: *My father's portrait* and *Aunt Letitia.* Thus the italicized clauses are not essential, only parenthetical; like any other parenthetical expressions (see 201E), they must be set off within commas.

Essential (restrictive) clauses. Omit commas around clauses that are essential to the meaning of the sentence— clauses that answer "which one(s)?":

> The portrait *that had hung in our hallway for years* was sold at auction. [tells which portrait]
> It was painted by an aunt *who had studied art in Paris.* [tells which aunt]

Without the italicized clauses, the above sentences could refer to any portrait or aunt:

> The portrait was sold at auction.
> It was painted by an aunt.

Thus the italicized clauses are essential, not merely parenthetical. They restrict the meaning of *portrait* and *aunt;* they answer the question "which one?"

Remember: Nonessential = commas
Essential = no commas

> **Note:** To tell whether a clause is essential, try the *that*-test: Adjective clauses beginning with *that* are always essential; also, if you can change *who* or *which* to *that* and still sound right, you have an essential clause:
> **Essential:** It was painted by an aunt *who* [or *that*] *had studied art in Paris.* [*That* sounds right.]
> **Nonessential:** It was painted by Aunt Letitia, *who* [but not *that*] *had studied art in Paris.* [*That* sounds wrong.]

> **Note:** In U.S. usage, *that* is generally preferred over *which* to begin an essential clause: The team *that* [rather than *which*] finishes fifth will miss the playoffs.

> **Note:** A *because* clause containing your point of emphasis is essential:
> The flag has thirteen stripes *because they represent the original thirteen states.* [emphasizes the reason; answers the question "Why does the flag have thirteen stripes?"]

A *because* clause giving information you consider merely incidental is nonessential:

> The flag has thirteen stripes, *because they represent the original thirteen states.* [answers the question "How many stripes does the flag have?" The reason here is only incidental.]

Nonessential phrases. Follow the principle for nonessential clauses (see above):

> **Nonessential:** Mayor Gibbs, *in his bright white suit,* spoke at the rally.
> **Essential:** The politician *in the bright white suit* spoke at the rally.

> **Nonessential:** Significantly more progress was made by the control group, *composed of five-year-olds.*
> **Essential:** Significantly more progress was made by the group *composed of five-year-olds.*

Nonessential appositives. Most appositives are nonessential, needing commas:

> Lola Palooza's newest film, *Grip of Fate,* opened at Cinema 65 last week.
> It earned $75 million nationwide, *a record amount.*
> My boyfriend, *a Yankee groundskeeper,* promised to get me Derek Jeter's autograph.

However, some appositives give essential information, answering "which one?" They take no commas:

> The film *Grip of Fate* earned $75 million last week. [appositive needed to tell which film]

Controlling your meaning. You control the meaning of your sentences when you use or omit commas, signaling nonessential or essential information:

> **Nonessential:** His sister, Paula, earned a Ph.D. [Commas show that we do not need to know the sister's name; thus he must have only one sister.]
> **Essential:** His sister Paula earned a Ph.D. [Omission of commas shows that Paula's name is essential, needed to identify which sister; thus he must have more than one sister.]

> **Nonessential:** Her friends, who live nearby, worried about her. [All her friends worried about her (and they all live nearby).]
> **Essential:** Her friends who live nearby worried about her. [Only some of her friends worried about her—the ones who live nearby.]

> **Nonessential:** Students, required to use the distant parking lot, are protesting to the dean. [All students are protesting (they all must use the distant lot).]
> **Essential:** Students required to use the distant parking lot are protesting to the dean. [Only certain students are protesting—those who must use the distant lot.]

See 202A for other examples of how commas change meaning.

201G. Absolute Phrases (see 124B, page 19, for definition):

> *The weather having turned chilly,* Bret donned his muffler.
> Shaunelle, *her confidence restored,* awaited the interview.

201H. Names or Other Words Used in Direct Address

> Tell us, *Marlene,* what solution you propose.
> *Mr. President,* may we quote you on that?

201I. *Yes* **and** *No* **at the Beginning of a Sentence**

> *Yes,* the lecture begins at noon.

201J. Mild Interjections (expressions of less than strong emotion):

> *Well,* perhaps it's better to wait.
> *Oh,* just put it down anywhere.

> *Note:* Strong interjections take an exclamation point: *Hey!* Come back with my purse. See 208, page 35.

201K. Direct Quotations. Generally, use a comma to set off a direct quotation (someone's exact words) from words that precede, follow, or interrupt it.

> "You may see the director now," said the secretary.
> "Haste," declares the proverb, "makes waste."

Punctuation of quotations is treated fully in 215–219, pages 38–39.

201L. Examples Introduced by *such as, especially, particularly;* **Expressions of Contrast**

> She excelled in many sports, *particularly* track.
> This department sells all kinds of footware, *such as* sneakers and hiking boots, for recreation.
> The letter is for Mom, *not* Dad.

> *Note:* Some *such as* phrases are essential, taking no commas: Résumés *such as this one* are thrown into the trash can.

202. Use a Comma Also

202A. Wherever Needed for Clarity, to prevent misreading. Omitting or misplacing needed commas can muddle or change your intended meaning:

> The story tells of Adele, an EMS worker who rescues nurses and then falls in love with Sven. [says she rescues nurses—not the intended meaning]
> The story tells of Adele, an EMS worker who rescues, nurses, and then falls in love with Sven. [She nurses Sven.]

> When he called Pat Hess heard the news. [unclear who heard]
> When he called Pat, Hess heard the news. [Hess heard]
> When he called, Pat Hess heard the news. [Pat heard]

> The Democrats said the Republicans were incompetent. [Republicans were incompetent.]
> The Democrats, said the Republicans, were incompetent. [Democrats were incompetent.]

Last month the Mortons took their third cruise to the Caribbean on the *Atlantic Princess*. [All three cruises were on that ship.]

Last month the Mortons took their third cruise to the Caribbean**,** on the *Atlantic Princess*. [Not all cruises were on that ship.]

The President's primary concern was to soothe the radicals in Congress who were clamoring for war without further delay. [Some radicals wanted war without delay.]

The President's primary concern was to soothe the radicals in Congress**,** who were clamoring for war**,** without further delay. [All the radicals wanted war; the President wanted to soothe them without delay.]

See also 201E, F, page 32.

202B. In Place of Omitted or Understood Words in structures such as

Math 301 was her first choice; *Math 308***,** *her second.* [or less formally, *Math 301 was her first choice, Math 308 her second.*]

202C. Before a Confirmatory (Tag) Question

The campus is safe after dark**,** *isn't it?*

202D. In Letters or Emails

After the greeting of a friendly letter or email: Dear Frank**,**

> *Note:* Use a colon in business correspondence: *Dear Mr. Coe:*

After the complimentary close in all correspondence: Very truly yours**,**

202E. In Dates and Addresses. In a month-day-year date, place the year within commas, as if it were parenthetical. Do the same with the state or country in an address:

In Skokie**,** *Illinois***,** on July 4**,** *2011***,** they were married.

> *Note:* Do not use a comma in a month-year or a day-month-year date or between a state and a ZIP code: May 2012; 6 June 1944; Phoenix, AZ 85032.

203. Do *Not* Use a Comma

203A. To Separate Subject and Verb or Verb and Completer

Wrong: Many reference *books,* *are* now online.
Right: Many reference *books are* now online.

Wrong: Municipal bonds *provide,* tax-free *income.*
Right: Municipal bonds *provide* tax-free *income.*

203B. To Join Two Independent Clauses

Wrong: A water main has burst, the street is closed. [This error is called a comma splice; see 129B, page 26.]

Join independent clauses with *and, but, or, nor, for, yet, so* (conjunctions), or a semicolon:

Right: A water main has burst**,** *and* the street is closed.
Right: A water main has burst**;** the street is closed.

203C. If No Comma Is Needed. Do not overload your sentences with commas. Use only those necessary for clarity, pace, or emphasis.

> *Wrong:* Today, just before noon, the new President, and his entourage, will appear in the doorway of the Capitol, to the strains of "Hail to the Chief," and process toward the Inaugural platform, to begin a new administration, with the good wishes of the nation. [eight commas]

> *Right:* Today just before noon[,] the new President and his entourage will appear in the doorway of the Capitol to the strains of "Hail to the Chief" and process toward the Inaugural platform to begin a new administration[,] with the good wishes of the nation. [no commas, or perhaps one or two]

For resources to help you master this section's topics, log in to www.mywritinglab.com and select Commas from the list of subtopics.

204–205. The Period [.]

204. Use a Period

204A. After Every Sentence Except a Direct Question or an Exclamation

The party is at Sutter's tonight**.** [declarative sentence]
Be there by nine**.** [imperative sentence]
I'll ask Carla how she's getting there**.** [indirect question (a question rephrased in declarative form); the direct question is "Carla, how are you getting there?"]

204B. After an Abbreviation or Initial

Mr., Mrs., U.S., Dr., Calif., M.D., Rev., lb.

> *Note:* You may write *Ms.* either with or without a period, so long as you are consistent. *Miss* never takes a period.

Do *not* use a period with

- Many well-known sets of initials: IBM, FBI, NBC, NASA, UN, YWCA, CD-ROM
- Postal abbreviations of states: MI, AZ, OR
- Radio and television stations: WSQK
- Money in even-dollar denominations: $40
- Contractions: ass'n, sec'y (for *association, secretary.* They may also be written as abbreviations: *assn., secy.*)
- Ordinal numbers: 5th, 2nd, Henry VIII
- Nicknames: Rob, Pat, Sid, Pam
- Common shortened terms: memo, math, exam, lab, gym (All these terms are colloquial; use the full words in formal writing.)

204C. After a Number or Letter in a Formal Outline

   1. Major stringed instruments
      A. Violin
      B. Cello

But do *not* use a period

- If the number or letter is within parentheses: (1), (a)
- If the number is part of a title: Chapter 4

204D. In a Spaced Group of Three (. . .) to Show

Ellipsis (the intentional omission of words) in a quoted passage. Retain necessary punctuation preceding the ellipsis:

> George V. Higgins has written, "I think the only way to find out whether the story in your mind is any good is to sit down by yourself and try to put all of it on paper. . . . If the story interests you enough, . . . it will interest other people."

The first of the four periods after *paper* signals the end of the sentence. Follow this practice whether the omission is before or after such a period.

If both you and the original author have used spaced periods, enclose your ellipsis in brackets. See example in 215F note, page 38.

Pause, hesitation, and the like in dialogue and interrupted narrative (do not overuse this device):

> This room. Yes, this room. . . . You . . . was it you? . . . were going out to look for something. . . . The tree of knowledge, wasn't it?
>
> —J. M. Barrie

204E. After a Nonsentence. A nonsentence is a legitimate unit of expression lacking subject + verb. It is found mostly in dialogue.

A greeting: Good evening**.**

A mild exclamation not within a sentence:

> Oh**.**   Darn**.**

An answer to a question: Will you accept? *Perhaps***.**

> *Note:* A nonsentence is a correct expression. A fragment (a similar structure *un*intentionally lacking subject + verb) is an error. See 129A, page 26.

205. Do *Not* Use a Period after a title at the head of a paper, even if that title is a sentence:

> The Benefits of Resuming Moon Exploration
> Exploring the Moon Again Can Yield Benefits

Do, however, use a question mark or exclamation point where appropriate in a title:

> Is Resuming Moon Exploration Worthwhile**?**

For resources to help you master this section's topics, log in to www.mywritinglab.com and select Final Punctuation *from the list of subtopics.*

206–207. The Question Mark [?]

206. Use a Question Mark

206A. After a Direct Question

> Did you get a call**?** When**?** From whom**?**
> It was from Mr. Ward, wasn't it**?**
> You testified earlier—do you recall**?**—that you didn't know him.
> You met him at a party**?** [A question may be in declarative-sentence form; the question mark signals the tone in which it would be spoken.]

For use of the question mark in quotations, see 218C, page 39; in titles, see 205.

206B. Within Parentheses to Indicate Doubt or Uncertainty

> Joan of Arc was born in 1412**(?)** and died in 1431.

207. Do *Not* Use a Question Mark

207A. After an Indirect Question (see 204A, page 34, for definition):

> Senator Henry asked what the program would cost.

207B. After a Polite Request in Question Form

> Would you please sign the enclosed papers.

207C. Within Parentheses to Express Humor or Irony

> *Wrong:* That purple suit shows his exquisite (?) taste. The words alone should suffice.

208–209. The Exclamation Point [!]

208. Use an Exclamation Point after a strong interjection or an emphatic sentence:

> Never**!**   He has a gun**!**
> How gross**!**   What a night**!**

For use of the exclamation point in titles, see 205. For its use in quotations, see 218C, page 39.

209. Do *Not* Use an Exclamation Point

209A. After a Mild Interjection or Mild Emotional Expression. The exclamation point loses its effect if overused. Except in quoted dialogue, reserve the exclamation point mostly for expressions that begin with *what* or *how* (and are not questions). Elsewhere, use the less dramatic comma or period:

> What a fool I was**!**   Why, I never knew that.

209B. More than Once, or with Other Pause or Stop Marks

> *Wrong:* That's a lie**!!!** [One *!* is sufficient.]
> *Wrong:* You failed again**?!** [Use either *?* or *!*.]

210. The Semicolon [;]

The semicolon signals a greater break in thought than the comma but less of a break than the period. It is, however, closer to a period than to a comma in most of its uses and is sometimes interchangeable with the period. The semicolon can give your writing a formal tone, as the examples below suggest.

210. Use a Semicolon

210A. Between Independent Clauses When There Is No Coordinating Conjunction

> The fifth edition contained thirty-two pages; by the eleventh edition, the book had grown to eighty pages.

The semicolon is particularly effective for showing balance or contrast between two clauses:

> The woods abound with wildlife; the lakes teem with fish.
>
> Freshmen think they know nothing; sophomores know they know everything.

210B. Between Independent Clauses Joined by a Conjunctive Adverb (*therefore, however, nevertheless, thus, moreover, also, besides, consequently, meanwhile, otherwise, then, furthermore, likewise, in fact, still*):

> Michael was an all-star in college basketball; *however,* he proved too small for professional ball.
>
> Asian factory workers are generally paid much less than American workers; *consequently,* many American wholesalers buy their manufactured goods overseas.

> *Note:* The comma after some conjunctive adverbs is optional.

Even when the conjunctive adverb drifts into the second clause, the semicolon stays put between the clauses:

> Michael was an all-star in college basketball; he proved too small, *however,* for professional ball.

210C. To Replace the Main Comma(s) Among Other Commas

Between independent clauses containing internal commas:

> Today we take for granted automobile safety equipment such as air bags, collapsible steering columns, and antilock brakes; *yet* sixty years ago cars were not required even to have directional signals, seat belts, or outside rearview mirrors. [The semicolon marks the break between the independent clauses more clearly than another comma would.]

In a series, between items containing internal commas:

> The new officers are Verna Brooks, chairperson; Pedro Lopez, social director; Sam Lee, treasurer; and Sharon Grady, secretary.

211–213. The Apostrophe [']

211. Use an Apostrophe with Possessive Nouns.

Possessive nouns show "belonging to." If your cousin has (possesses) a new laptop, we say it is your cousin**'s** laptop; it belongs to her. *Cousin's* is a possessive noun. An apostrophe and a final *s* sound are the signals of possession.

> *Note:* **To tell whether a noun is possessive,** try saying it at the end of an *of* phrase. For example, which is correct: *the teacher house, the teachers house,* or *the teacher's house?* Say to yourself *the house of the teacher.* If that is what you mean, then *teacher* is possessive and *the teacher's house* is correct.

211A. Singular Nouns. To make a singular noun possessive, add **'s**: a boy**'s** life [the life of a boy], Charles Jones**'s** career [the career of Charles Jones], Ms. Huang**'s** cats, a bear**'s** trail, a goalie**'s** equipment, a fox**'s** lair, the class**'s** behavior.

Exception: Omit the *s* on many classical and Biblical names that already end in *s:* Ulysses' travels, Sophocles' irony, Jesus' teachings.

> *Note:* Some authorities favor not adding the *s* to any nouns that already end in *s:* Jones' career, the class' behavior. Whichever style you choose, be consistent.

211B. Plural Nouns. Since most plurals already end in *s,* add only an apostrophe to make them possessive: the two boys' lives [the lives of the two boys], the Joneses' careers [the careers of the Joneses], the Huangs' cats, the bears' trail, the goalies' equipment, the foxes' lair, both classes' behavior.

For the few plurals that do not end in *s,* use **'s**: women**'s** rights [the rights of women], the people**'s** voice, the geese**'s** flight.

Caution: Do not mistake ordinary plural nouns (the *cats* are fed; I know the *Huangs*) or verbs ending in *s* (she *runs* fast) for possessives. See 213B, page 37.

211C. Possessives Before Gerunds (Verbal Nouns). Just as you would say *Marissa's action surprised us,* say *Marissa's resigning surprised us* and *We were surprised by Marissa's sudden resigning without any reason.* Other examples: *The UN protested the rebels' constant firing upon the refugees. The townspeople were opposed to the tavern's staying open all night.*

But if the possessive sounds awkward (as when modifiers follow it), omit it: *The townspeople were opposed to the tavern that played loud music staying open all night.*

211D. Fine Points of Possession

Joint vs. individual possession. If two or more nouns possess something jointly, only the last noun gets an apostrophe:

> *Mary and Bill's wedding is next Saturday.*

If each noun possesses a separate thing, each noun gets its own apostrophe:

Both Mary's and Bill's parents will attend.

Hyphenated words. Add the apostrophe to the last word only:

Her *sister-in-law's* illness prevents her from attending.

Possessive pronouns can be confusing. Possessive **indefinite** and **reciprocal** pronouns take an apostrophe, just like nouns: any*body's, someone's, each other's, one another's, someone else's, everybody else's*… (see 121D, page 16, for a full list). But possessive **personal** pronouns never take an apostrophe: *his, hers, its, ours, yours, theirs;* nor does *whose. Its* and *whose,* particularly, cause problems because they look much like the contractions for *it is* and *who is* (see 212A and 213A; 122F, page 18; and 404, pages 54–59).

Words expressing time or amount form their possessives just as other nouns do: *a dollar's worth, a moment's rest, a week's pay, two weeks' pay.*

Understood nouns. If you omit a noun to avoid repetition, be sure to keep the apostrophe on any preceding possessive:

Wrong: Katelyn's essay was clearer than Daves.
Right: Katelyn's essay was clearer than Dave's. [than Dave's essay]

See 211E.

211E. Apostrophes and Clarity. An omitted or misplaced apostrophe can convey the wrong meaning. Each sentence below is the same except for an apostrophe, yet each has a different meaning:

After talking about her health, she discussed her daughters. [her daughters in general, not just their health]

After talking about her health, she discussed her daughter's. [the health of one daughter]

After talking about her health, she discussed her daughters'. [the health of all her daughters]

212. Use an Apostrophe Also

212A. To Show Contractions and Other Omissions of Letters or Numerals

can't [cannot]	what's [what is]	it's [it is]
who's [who is]	we're [we are]	they're [they are]
you're [you are]	class of '15 [2015]	fishin' [fishing]

212B. To Form the Plurals of Letters and Symbols

Her grades included three *A*'s and two *B*'s.
Use +'s and -'s on the test.

Use the apostrophe only where clarity demands it. You generally do not need it with figures (the *1990s,* hitting in the .*300s*), words referred to as words (*ifs, ands,* or *buts*), or initials (*YWCAs*).

213. Do *Not* Use an Apostrophe

213A. With Possessive Personal Pronouns (*his, hers, its, ours, yours, theirs*) or with *whose*

Whose sales team has surpassed *its* quota? Is it *hers, yours,* or *theirs?* It could be *ours.* (See 122F, page 18, and 404, pages 54–59, for *its/it's,* etc.)

213B. With Ordinary Plurals or Verbs

The *Browns* went to the *stores.* Countless *stars* appeared. [ordinary plurals, not possessives]
The mayor *says* no, but she *means* perhaps. [verbs ending in s]

213C. To Form the Possessives of Most Inanimate Objects

Say *the sole of her shoe* (not *her shoe's sole*), *the top of the pile* (not *the pile's top*). But if the *of* phrase sounds awkward, use the possessive: *a week's pay* (not *the pay of a week*).

For resources to help you master this section's topics, log in to www.mywritinglab.com and select Apostrophes from the list of subtopics.

214. Italics (Underlining)

Italic type, or *italics,* is slanted type, like the first words of this sentence. In handwriting, indicate italics by underlining: <u>The Devil in the White City</u>. On a computer, use actual italics.

Note: Some magazines and newspapers follow styles that omit italics. Avoid such alternatives; follow standard style.

214. Use Italics to Designate

214A. Titles of Separate Publications

Books: Our readings include Fitzgerald's *Tender Is the Night.*

Magazines, newspapers, and journals: Lily enjoys reading both *Rolling Stone* and the *Wall Street Journal.*

Do not capitalize or italicize the word *the* in a newspaper or magazine title.

Bulletins, pamphlets, and newsletters:

County Conservation Tips

Plays, films, TV and radio programs, and musical productions:

The Phantom of the Opera [play or musical production]
The Social Network [film or DVD]
NCIS: Los Angeles [television or radio program. For a single episode in a series, use quotation marks: "The Missing Marine."]

Poems long enough to be published alone as books:

Homer's *Iliad*   Seamus Heaney's *Beowulf*

Electronic publications (tapes, CDs, DVDs, CD-ROMs, online databases...):

> *Britannica SmartMath*

> *Note:* Do not underline, italicize, or put in quotation marks the title at the head of a report, essay, or paper (unless the title contains words that would be italicized, etc. anyway, such as the title of a novel):
>
> Irony in Joseph Heller's Early Novels
> Irony in Heller's *Catch-22*

214B. Names of Ships, Trains, Aircraft, and Spacecraft

> The *Alaskan Explorer* embarked on her maiden voyage.
> The spacecraft *Apollo 11* took the first humans to the moon.

214C. Titles of Paintings and Sculptures

> *Morning Sun*   Michelangelo's *David*   *The Blue Boy*

214D. Foreign Words Not in an English Dictionary

> The lovers bade each other *sayonara*.

Generally, if a word is listed in a reputable English dictionary, it is considered Anglicized and needs no italics:

> They could not now stop the police raid; it was a fait accompli. [The last two words, French for "accomplished fact," are in Webster's.]

Do not italicize these common Latin abbreviations:

> a.m., p.m., A.D., viz., vs., etc., i.e., e.g.

214E. Words, Letters, Figures, or Symbols Referred to as Such

> Remember the *d* when spelling *supposed to*.
> His license number contained two *J*'s and a *9*.
> Avoid using *&* for *and* in formal writing.

214F. Emphasis, where you cannot convey it by the order or choice of your words:

> Ms. Coe said that she *might* reconsider the grade. [The emphasis on *might* stresses the uncertainty.]

Avoid overuse of italics for emphasis.

215–219. Quotation Marks [" "]

Quotation marks enclose the exact words of a speaker, certain titles, or words used in a special sense. Quotation marks are always (with one small exception) used in pairs.

215. Use Regular (Double) Quotation Marks [" "] to Enclose a Direct Quotation.

215A. Use Quotation Marks Around a Speaker's Exact Words. Note that commas set off each quotation:

> Professor Fossle declared, "Study chapter 7 for next class."
> "Study chapter 7 for next class," declared Professor Fossle.
> Professor Fossle said, "Study chapter 7," and left the room.

> *Note:* Do not use quotation marks with an *indirect* quotation (a paraphrase or summary of a speaker's words):
>
> Professor Fossle said that we should study chapter 7.

215B. With an Interrupted Quotation, use quotation marks around only the quoted words:

> "Study chapter 7," said Professor Fossle, "and be ready for a quiz."

215C. With an *Un*interrupted Quotation of More than One Sentence, use quotation marks only before the first sentence and after the last:

> **Wrong:** Professor Fossle said, "Study chapter 7." "There will be a quiz Monday."
>
> **Right:** Professor Fossle said, "Study chapter 7. There will be a quiz Monday."

215D. With an *Un*interrupted Quotation of Several Paragraphs, use either of the following forms:

- Put quotation marks at the beginning of each paragraph but at the end of only the last paragraph.
- Use no quotation marks at all; instead, type the entire quotation as an indented block. See 501B, page 60.

215E. With a Fragmentary Quotation (only a short part of a sentence), omit the comma(s):

> The warranty says it covers only "normal household use."

215F. Use Three Spaced Periods to Show Omission of unimportant or irrelevant words from a quotation (ellipsis—see 204D, page 35):

> Emerson wrote, "Is it so bad, then, to be misunderstood? ... To be great is to be misunderstood."

> *Note:* If you use ellipsis in a quotation that already has spaced periods, enclose your ellipsis in brackets (keep all the original punctuation in its proper place outside the brackets): "This room. Yes, this room. ... You [...] were going out to look for [...] the tree of knowledge, wasn't it?" Compare this with the full quotation in 204D, page 35.

215G. To Insert Your Explanatory Words into a Quotation, use brackets (not parentheses). See 225A, page 41.

215H. When Quoting Dialogue, start a new paragraph with each change of speaker:

> "The lead guitarist is superb," she whispered during the opening number.
> "He sounds tinny to me," I replied.

215I. When Quoting Poetry, use quotation marks only for very short passages (three lines or fewer) that are run into your text. Use a slash mark (with a space before and after) to show the end of each line of the poem:

> Emily Dickinson compares exultation to "the going / Of an inland soul to sea."

For quotations of more than three lines, do not use quotation marks; type the lines as an indented block as explained in 501B, page 60.

216. Use Double Quotation Marks Also to Enclose

216A. Titles of Short Written Works: Poems, Articles, Essays, Short Stories, Chapters, Songs

"Silence" is a short story in Alice Munro's book *Runaway*. Study "Finding a Topic" in Lester's *Writing Research Papers*. "Girls in Their Summer Clothes" is my favorite Bruce Springsteen song.

See 214A, page 37, for episodes of a TV series.

216B. Definitions of Words

The word *instance* means "a case or example."

216C. Words Used in a Special Sense or for a Special Purpose

[A]nti-drug agents detained two brothers accused of being . . . producers of methamphetamines, or "speed."
　　　　　　　　　　　　　　　—*New York Times*

If you are using the word several times within a chapter or short paper, you need quotation marks only the first time.

> *Note:* You do not need quotation marks around a slang expression or nickname: Chuckie Potts was truly a wuss.

217. Use Single Quotation Marks ['] to enclose a quotation within a quotation. Think of this construction as a box within a box. Ordinary double quotation marks [" "] provide the wrapping around the outer box; single quotation marks ['] provide the wrapping around the inner box. Be sure to place end punctuation within the correct box:

"I've said twice, 'All papers due Monday,'" Professor Fossle snapped.

218. Use Other Marks with Quotation Marks as Follows:

218A. Periods and Commas. In U.S. usage, always put these marks *inside* closing quotation marks:

"I want facts," said Professor Fossle, "not fantasies."

218B. Colons and Semicolons. Always put these marks *outside* closing quotation marks:

Professor Fossle said, "I'm an easy grader"; however, my paper failed.
Three of us penned "An Ode to Professor Fossle": Simms, Romero, and I.

218C. Question Marks, Exclamation Points, and Dashes.

Place these marks *inside* the quotation marks when they belong to the quotation, *outside* otherwise:

Earl asked, "Which way is the arena?" [The quotation is the question.]

Did Earl say, "I know the way"? [The part outside the quotation is the question.]
Did Earl ask, "Which way is the arena"? [Both the quotation and the outside part are questions. Use only one question mark—the outside one.]
"We're lost!" Earl exclaimed.
How angry I felt when Earl said, "We'll be late for the game"!
"I think we should—" I began, but Earl was not listening.
"There"—Earl pointed ahead—"is someone we can ask."

219. Do *Not* Use Quotation Marks

219A. Around a Title at the Head of a Paper, including essays, reports, and creative pieces (unless the title is a quotation):

Wrong: "The Electric Car: Problems and Solutions"
Right: The Electric Car: Problems and Solutions

219B. To Show Intended Irony, Humor, or Emphasis. Your irony or humor will be more effective if not so blatantly pointed out:

Wrong: His "golden" voice emptied the opera house.
Right: His golden voice emptied the opera house.

For emphasis, use italics (see 214F, page 38.)

For resources to help you master this section's topics, log in to www.mywritinglab.com and select Quotation Marks from the list of subtopics.

220–221. The Colon [:]

220. Use a Colon to Introduce

220A. A List That Follows a Grammatically Complete Statement. (Think of the colon as meaning "and here they are" or "and here it is.") The list is usually in apposition to a preceding noun in the statement:

The President's itinerary included four East Asian nations: India, Indonesia, Japan, and South Korea. [The four names are in apposition to *nations*.]
One nation was bypassed: North Korea. [*North Korea* is in apposition to *nation*.]

Often *the following* or *as follows* precedes the colon:

The President's itinerary included the following: India, Indonesia, Japan, and South Korea.

> *Note:* Use *the following* and *as follows* sparingly; often they can be avoided: The President's itinerary included India, Indonesia, Japan, and South Korea.

Do not use a colon after an *in*complete statement (one that lacks, for example, a needed verb completer), or after *such as* or *for example:*

Wrong: The itinerary included: India, Indonesia, Japan, and South Korea.
Right: The itinerary included India, Indonesia....

Wrong: The itinerary included nations such as: India, Indonesia, and Japan.

Right: The itinerary included nations such as India, Indonesia, and Japan.

(Exception: see 220B, C.)

220B. A Long Quotation (one or more paragraphs):

In *The Sketch Book* Washington Irving wrote:

> English travelers are the best and the worst in the world. Where no motives of pride or interest intervene, none can equal them. . . . [Quotation continues for one or more paragraphs.]

220C. A Formal Quotation or Question

Cutting the tape, the governor declared: "The Greenport-Springview Bridge is officially open."

The basic question is: Where is our country headed?

(See 301D, page 43, on when to capitalize after a colon.)

220D. A Second Independent Clause That Explains or Illustrates the First Clause

On our Southwest trip we came upon several unexpected delights: Carlsbad Caverns, for one, proved breathtaking.

220E. The Body of a Business Letter or Email (after the greeting)

Dear Madam: Dear Dr. Flynn:

> **Note:** Use a comma after the greeting of a personal (friendly) letter. See 202D, page 34.

220F. The Details Following an Announcement

For rent: room with kitchen, near campus.

220G. A Formal Resolution, After the Word *Resolved*

Resolved: That the club spend $50 for decorations.

220H. The Words of a Speaker in a Play (after the speaker's name):

FALSTAFF: Sixteen at least, my lord.

221. Use a Colon to Separate

221A. Parts of a Title, Reference, or Numeral

Title: *The Cold War: A Reinterpretation*
Reference: Isaiah 10:3–15 [but in MLA style, *10.3–15*]
Numeral: 11:25 p.m.

221B. Certain Parts of a Bibliography Entry. See section 509, pages 70–74, for full details. Here are two common uses:

Book (between names of city and publisher):

Sobel, Dava. *Galileo's Daughter: A Historical Memoir of Science, Faith, and Love.* New York: Walker, 1999.

Article (between date and page numbers):

"Where to Shop." *Consumer Reports* Aug. 2010: 12–15.

For resources to help you master this section's topics, log in to www.mywritinglab.com and select Semicolons, Colons, Dashes, and Parentheses from the list of subtopics.

222. The Dash [—]

The dash signals an abrupt break in the flow of a sentence. Do not use it for an ordinary pause or stop in place of a comma, period, or semicolon. When keyboarding, make a dash by using two strokes of the hyphen key, with no spaces before, between, or after, like this:--.

222. Use a Dash

222A. To Show a Sudden Break in Thought

I left it right here in the—well, I guess I didn't.

This room is so quiet it—what was that noise?

"My dear constituents, I greet you—" the senator began, but he was stopped by a chorus of boos.

222B. To Set Off a Parenthetical Element that is long, that sharply interrupts the sentence, or that otherwise would be hard to distinguish:

Passengers now had to present two forms of identification—current passport, driver's license, original birth certificate, or identification card with photograph—before being allowed to board planes or even enter the terminal.

Our old car—it must know when we're in a hurry—again refused to start.

Above the door hung a portrait—gilt-framed but cracked, peeling, and tilted—of a bewigged gentleman in Colonial dress.

222C. To Emphasize or Clarify an Appositive

He had only one goal—stardom. [You may use a colon instead if the appositive ends a sentence: He had only one goal: stardom. The colon is more formal than the dash.]

Sarah, Vera, Maria, Tammy—all have found better jobs.

Three majors—literature, writing, and linguistics—are offered in this department.

222D. To Precede the Author's Name After a Direct Quotation

Good breeding consists in concealing how much we think of ourselves and how little we think of the other person.

—Mark Twain

223–224. Parentheses [( )]

223. Use Parentheses (Always in Pairs)

223A. To Set Off Incidental Information or Comments

Senator Claghorn (D., Colorado) opposed the tax bill.

Her novel is set in Tuscany (we know the area well) and depicts the region's rural family life.

Note: Do not overuse parentheses. Use commas to set off ordinary parenthetical (interrupting) expressions (see 201E, page 32). Do not use an opening capital letter or closing period with a sentence in parentheses within a larger sentence (see second example above).

223B. To Enclose

Letters or figures in enumeration:

To complete the loan application, you need to **(1)** provide your Social Security number, **(2)** choose a repayment period, and **(3)** have your signature notarized.

References and directions:

The amoeba **(**see figure 6**)** reproduces asexually.

A question mark indicating uncertainty:

She was born in China in 1778**(?)** and died in 1853.

Certain information in bibliographies and citations:

McNamara, J. **(**Ed.**)**. **(**2004**)**. *The Irish face in America.* New York: Bulfinch. [APA style]

See sections 508A, page 69, and 509, pages 70–74, for details of citation and bibliographic form.

223C. For Accuracy, in Legal Documents and Business Correspondence

Please remit the sum of fifty dollars **(**$50**)**.

223D. With Other Punctuation Marks as Follows:

The comma, semicolon, and period follow the closing parenthesis in a sentence:

Her latest novel is set in Tuscany **(**she has lived there since 2003**)**, but she plans to set her next one in Venice.
The bill was supported in the Senate by Sam Harlan **(**R., Texas**)**; it was championed in the House by Meghan Marsh **(**D., Minnesota**)**.

The question mark and the exclamation point go inside the parentheses if the mark belongs to the parenthetical element; otherwise, they go outside:

The book mentions Mechthild of Magdeburg **(**died 1282**?)**.
Have you read much of Samuel Butler **(**died 1680**)?**
Sid asked me to lend him fifty dollars **(**what nerve**!)**.

224. Do *Not* Use Parentheses

224A. To Indicate Deletions. Instead, draw a line through the deleted words:

Wrong: Summer Olympics were held in (2010) 2012.
Right: Summer Olympics were held in ~~2010~~ 2012.

224B. To Enclose Your Own Comment Within a Quotation. Use brackets for this purpose; see 225A and 225A note.

225. Brackets [[ ]]

225. Use Brackets

225A. To Enclose Your Own Editorial or Explanatory Comment Within a Direct Quotation

In his autobiography Foster Fenwick declares, "I discovered the wonder drug Flossicam while puttering in my lab in 2006 [the AMA disputes this claim] and tested it rigorously before applying for a patent."

Note: Some newspapers use parentheses instead of brackets. Do not follow their style.

See 215F, page 38, for use of brackets with ellipses in quotations.

225B. Around *sic* to Mark a Quoted Writer's Error. *Sic* is Latin for "thus it is." Use it to show that an error in material you are quoting is not yours but the original writer's:

"Police have been questioning the principle [sic] suspect for days," the local newspaper stated.

225C. To Enclose Stage Directions

JUAN [striding to the door]: Someone must help them.

225D. For Parenthetical Remarks Within Outer Parentheses

Steps in applying (labeled 1–7 [pages 4a–4d] on your list) must be followed in sequence.

Wherever possible, avoid such complication by recasting the sentence:

In applying, follow steps labeled 1–7 (pages 4a–4d) in sequence.

226. The Hyphen [-]

226. Use a Hyphen

226A. To Join Certain Compound Words

sister-in-law   will-o'-the-wisp   Scotch-Irish

A good dictionary will show which compounds are hyphenated. Generally, if the compound is not in the dictionary, write it as two words, with no hyphen: *tree trunk.*

226B. To Join Words Used as a Single Adjective before a noun:

a well-known author   late-model cars   fifty-dollar bill
a now-you-see-me-now-you-don't office presence
cat-and-mouse game

Ordinarily, do not hyphenate such words when they do not precede nouns:

Hanley is *well known*. It was a game of *cat and mouse*.

Do not use a hyphen between an *-ly* adverb and an adjective: *freshly baked* bread [not *freshly-baked* bread].

With a series of hyphenated modifiers, omit the part after the hyphen until the last item: The drawer contained *ten-*, *twenty-*, and *fifty-dollar* bills.

226C. With Two-Word Numbers and Fractions

thirty-three   ninety-eighth   four-fifths

Additional words in the number take no hyphen:

four hundred twenty-five   five twenty-fourths

See 305–307, pages 45–46, for complete number-writing rules.

Hyphenate a compound adjective containing a number:

ten-year-old boy   forty-hour week

hundred-yard dash   ten-dollar bill

two- and three-room apartments

226D. To Clarify Meaning

Wrong: Amy was the *third prize winner*. [*third winner* or *third prize?*]

Right: Amy was the *third prize-winner*. [third person to win a prize]

Right: Amy was the *third-prize winner*. [winner of the prize for third place]

Wrong: Dr. Doris Wertheim, an *adolescent disease specialist* at Municipal Hospital, diagnosed Lucy's condition. [Was the doctor a teenager?]

Right: Dr. Doris Wertheim, an *adolescent-disease specialist* at Municipal Hospital, diagnosed Lucy's condition.

Observe the difference within each pair:

a great grandfather [a grandfather who is admired]
a great-grandfather [a grandfather's father]

an unfinished furniture store [a furniture store not fully built]
an unfinished-furniture store [a store selling unpainted furniture]

more recent films [additional recent films]
more-recent films [films made more recently]

226E. With *ex-* ("Former"), *self-*, *all-*, *-elect*, and *-designate*

ex-manager   self-pity

all-county   Mayor-elect Bobbs

Secretary-designate Reynolds

When adding most other prefixes or suffixes or combining short roots, do not hyphenate: *cooperate, coworker, antiterrorist, nonunion, semiliterate, bimonthly, multinational, citywide*. But keep the hyphen where

- the root is capitalized: *anti-American, Europe-wide*
- ambiguity could result: *recover* [to get back] vs. *re-cover* [to cover again]; *recreation* [enjoyable activity] vs. *re-creation* [creating again]
- awkwardness would result: *semi-independent*, to avoid an awkward double *i*.

226F. To Show Spelled-out Words, Hesitation, or Stammering

"I'm buying some i-c-e c-r-e-a-m," the child's mother told her husband.

"It's c-c-cold in h-here," the old man stammered.

226G. To Divide Overlong Words at the End of Lines

Urban leaders, advocates for the poor, liberals, traditionalists, and environmentalists all praised the new law.

> *Note:* Put the hyphen at the end of the first line, never at the beginning of the second line. Do not guess where a word should divide; consult your dictionary. See 304, page 45, for more details on word division.

227. The Slash [/]

227. Use a Slash (not a backward slash [\])

227A. Between Lines of Poetry Quoted in Running Text

Elizabeth Barrett Browning wrote in a sonnet, "If thou must love me, let it be for naught / Except for love's sake only." [Leave a space before and after the slash.]

For longer quotations of poetry, see 501B, page 60.

227B. Between Alternatives

To reach Baltimore, take the Maryland Turnpike/Interstate 95 [alternative names for the same road].

Do not use a slash for a hyphen: St. Louis-Denver [not St. Louis/Denver] flights. For and/or, see 402C, page 52.

227C. With Certain Figures: $1.65/lb, 5/8 [five eighths], x/2.

Our written language requires attention to several types of details, such as capitalization and number form, that spoken language does not. Such kinds of details are called **mechanics.** Your attention to the mechanics of writing, including spelling, signals your reader that you are a careful writer, concerned about your paper's readability and clarity.*

301–303. Capitalization

301. Capitalize

301A. The First Word of Every Sentence, including quoted sentences:

> **T**he salesperson promised, "**T**his car will absolutely never give you trouble."

But do *not* capitalize the first word of

An indirect quotation (paraphrase): The salesperson promised *that the car would never give me trouble.*

A fragmentary quotation: The salesperson promised that the car would "**a**bsolutely never" give me trouble.

A sentence in parentheses within another sentence: The salesperson promised (**h**e must have had his fingers crossed) that the car would never give me trouble.

This last rule applies also between dashes; see 222B, page 40.

301B. The First Word of a Line of Poetry (unless the poet has used lowercase [small] letters):

> **W**henever Richard Cory went down town,
> **W**e people on the pavement looked at him:
> **H**e was a gentleman from sole to crown,
> **C**lean favored, and imperially slim.
> —Edwin Arlington Robinson

301C. Words and Phrases Used as Sentences

> **W**here?　　**N**ever.　　**N**o, not you.　　**O**f course.

301D. The First Word of a Formal Question or Statement Following a Colon

> The debate centered on a vital question: **W**here is the borderline between individual freedom and national security? Hemingway said it best: **C**ourage is grace under pressure.

Use lowercase, however, for ordinary statements following colons:

> There was a reason for his behavior: **h**e was in love.

301E. The First Word of Each Item in a Formal Outline

> I. **T**ypes of Sentences
> 　A. **S**imple
> 　B. **C**ompound

301F. Most Words in a Title of a book, short story, film, play, article, chapter, song, and the like:

> *The New Biographical Dictionary of Film* [book]
> "**T**ime to **S**tart **O**ver" [article]

Always capitalize the first and the last word. Capitalize the first word following a dash or colon in a title:

> *Cleopatra: A Life*

---

*Other elements of mechanics are treated elsewhere: punctuation in Part 2, manuscript form in section 501.

Capitalize all other words *except*

Articles (*a, an, the*):
> *The Day of **t**he Locust*

Prepositions (*on, in, to . . .*) and *to* in an infinitive:
> *Swimming **in** a Sea of Death*　　*A Night **to** Remember*

Coordinating conjunctions (*and, but, or…*):
> *The Sound **a**nd the Fury*

Caution: Do not assume that all short words in titles are lowercased; short verbs and pronouns, for example, follow the capitalization rule: "Where **Is** My Love?"; *Some Like **It** Hot.*

> ***Note:*** Some authorities favor capitalizing prepositions of five or more letters, such as *about: Much **A**do **A**bout Nothing.*
> 　　Most authorities favor not capitalizing (or italicizing) *the* before a newspaper or magazine title: The story was in the *San Francisco Chronicle.*

301G. In a Letter or Email, Key Words in the Greeting and Close. Capitalize the first and last words in the greeting, or salutation (***My** dearest **Son***), but only the first word in the complimentary close (***Very** truly yours*).

301H. The Pronoun *I* and the Interjection *O* (but not *oh*):

> To thee, **O** Lord, **I** pray.　　Why, **oh** why?

302. Capitalize Proper Nouns.
A proper noun, as distinguished from a common noun, is the name of a specific person, place, or thing: *Shakespeare, America, Eiffel Tower.* (A proper adjective, made from a proper noun, is also capitalized: *Shakespearean, American.*) Do not capitalize *the* before such nouns: *the Snake River, the Ming Dynasty, the Department of Sanitation.*

Proper Noun	Common Noun
Angela	woman
Seattle	city
October	month
Whitttier College	school
Dallas Elks Club	organization

302A. Specific Persons, Ethnic Groups, Tribes, Nationalities, Religions, and Languages

Chelsea Clinton	Hispanic	Navajo
Malaysian	Buddhist	Flemish

> ***Note:*** Most authorities, though not all, favor lowercasing *black, white, aborigine,* and other racial descriptions. Whichever style you choose, be consistent with all races.

302B. Specific Places (countries, states, cities, geographic sections; oceans, lakes, and other bodies of water; streets, buildings, rooms, parks, monuments, and so forth):

Myanmar	Arctic Ocean	South Main Street
North Carolina	Pacific Rim	Barr Building
Santa Barbara	Room 67	Lake Superior
Prospect Park	Vietnam Memorial	

Lakes Erie and Huron (but *the Mississippi and Missouri rivers*)

302C. Specific Organizations, Companies, and Brand Names

White Sox	United Nations	Board of Health
Lutheran Church	Red Cross	Yoho Ski Club
Democratic Party	Supreme Court	Ace Tire Corp.

Hewlett Packard computers [Lowercase the product.]

302D. Days of the Week, Months, Holidays, and Holy Days

Friday	April	Fourth of July	Mother's Day
Labor Day	Easter	Yom Kippur	Ramadan

302E. Religious Names Considered Sacred

God (but *the gods*)   the Almighty   the Virgin   Allah

> *Note:* The modern tendency is not to capitalize pronouns referring to the Deity except to avoid ambiguity: *Trust in Him.* But *God showed his mercy.*

302F. Historical Events, Periods, and Documents

Vietnam War	Battle of Stalingrad
Great Depression	Renaissance
Magna Carta	Civil Rights Act

But *twentieth century, feminist movement, mysticism*

302G. Educational Institutions, Departments, Specific Courses, Classes of Students, and Specific Academic Degrees

Duke University	Economics 101 [but see 303D]	Department of Music
Senior Class	Ph.D.	

302H. Flags, Awards, and School Colors

Stars and Stripes	Grammy Award
Nobel Prize	Blue and Gold

302I. Stars and Planets

North Star	Jupiter	Big Dipper

> *Note:* Do not capitalize *sun* and *moon* unless they are personified (considered as persons). Do not capitalize *earth* unless it is personified or considered as one of the planets: The balloonists returned to Mother Earth. Venus and Mars are the closest planets to Earth.

302J. Ships, Trains, Aircraft, and Spacecraft

U.S.S. *Intrepid*   *Silver Meteor*   *Endeavour*

302K. Initials and Other Letter Combinations indicating time, divisions of government, letter equivalents of telephone numbers, call letters of radio and television stations, and certain other well-known letter combinations:

B.C. [or B.C.E.]	DVD	1-800-BUY HERE
FBI	O.K. [or OK]	AIDS
KMOX	A.D. [or C.E.]	CBS

302L. Personifications

Mother Nature   Old Man Winter   the hand of Death

302M. Titles Preceding Names

Professor Harold Hill	Chief Justice Roberts
Colonel Flagg	the Reverend Graham

Do not capitalize a title *following* a name unless the title shows very high national or international distinction:

Harold Hill, professor of music
Elizabeth II, Queen of Great Britain

You may capitalize a title of very high distinction when used instead of the person's name. Be consistent in this usage:

The President greeted the Pope.

Capitalize an abbreviated title before or after a name:

Prof. Sarah Sheldon, Ph.D.   Sen. Homer Page, Jr.

303. Do *Not* Capitalize

303A. Points of the Compass

The trail led north by northwest.

But do capitalize such words when referring to sections of the nation or world (usually preceded by *the*):

States in the West and Southeast are gaining population.
The Middle East's perspective differs from the West's.

303B. Names of Seasons (unless personified):

The South is warm in winter, hot in summer.

. . . crown old Winter's head with flowers.
　　　　　　　　　　　　　　　—Richard Crashaw

303C. Words Denoting Family Relationships when they follow a possessive noun or pronoun:

She is Jorge's aunt.   My father has just left.

But do capitalize when using the family relationship as a title preceding a name or by itself as a name:

Jorge greeted Aunt Julia.   Come back, Father.

303D. Names of Academic Disciplines (unless they are part of specific course titles or proper nouns):

Courses in psychology and sociology are crowded.
The college offers Psychology 101 and Sociology 203. [specific course titles]
Courses in Latin and Greek are also available. [proper nouns]

303E. Common Nouns (unless they are part of proper nouns):

The **f**ire **d**epartment from an **u**pstate **c**ounty won the **f**ire-fighting **c**ontest at the local **h**igh **s**chool.

The **M**ayfield **F**ire **B**rigade from **F**ulton **C**ounty won the **A**ll-**N**ortheast **F**irefighters' **C**ontest at **N**orthville **H**igh **S**chool.

303F. Common Words Derived from Proper Nouns

french fries   **c**hina [dishes]   **r**oman numerals

303G. The First Word After a Semicolon

She wanted to travel; **h**e wanted to stay put.

303H. The First Word in the Latter Part of an Interrupted Quotation (unless that word begins a new sentence):

"English 405," Ralph insisted, "**w**ill do wonders for your writing." [All quoted words are one sentence.]

"Take English 405," Ralph insisted. "**I**t will do wonders for your writing." [*It* begins a new quoted sentence.]

303I. The First Word of a Fragmentary Quotation (one that is only part of a sentence):

Her courage was called "**a**bove and beyond duty."

303J. The Second Part of Most Hyphenated Words (unless the second part is a proper noun):

Twenty-**t**hird Street   Governor-**e**lect Upshaw

Secretary-**d**esignate Rhoda Rew   anti-**A**merican

303K. A Word That You Want to Emphasize (use italics instead):

Wrong: You were told NOT to plagiarize.

Right: You were told *not* to plagiarize.

303L. Words for Parts of a Literary Work—such as *section, preface, appendix, bibliography, page, chapter, act, scene, stanza*—within sentences:

I read **c**hapter 4 and checked the **i**ndex and **a**ppendix.

For resources to help you master this section's topics, log in to www.mywritinglab.com and select Capitalization from the list of subtopics.

304. Word Division (Syllabication)

In computer keyboarding, words that do not fit at the end of a typed line are automatically moved to the next line. Nevertheless, you need to know word-division principles for other writing occasions, such as handwritten examinations or letters.

General principles: Avoid dividing any words if possible; try especially not to break words on two successive lines. When you must break a word, end the first part with a hyphen (made with one keyboard stroke [-] with no space before it). Do not have the hyphen begin the next line.

A good dictionary is your most reliable guide to hyphenation; remembering the following rules, however, will mean fewer trips to the dictionary.

304A. Divide According to Pronunciation; Always Divide Between Syllables. Leave enough of a word at the end of the first line to suggest the sound and meaning of the whole word: *incen-diary* (better than *in-cendiary*), *irregular, change-able.*

304B. Divide Compound Words Between the Parts: *handbook, book-keeper, rattle-snake.* If a compound word is already hyphenated, break it at an existing hyphen: *sister-in-law, self-portrait, twenty-one-month* lease.

304C. Do Not Divide a One-Syllable Word of Any Length.

thoughts, straight, clashed, twelfths, screeched

304D. Do Not Set Off a Single Letter as a Syllable.

Wrong: a-part, dough-y   **Right:** apart, doughy

305–307. Numbers

305. In Sentences, Generally Write a Number in Words When

305A. The Number Contains Only One or Two Words.

thirty days, *sixty-three* chapters, *six hundred* members, *twenty-seventh* floor

> **Note:** Some publishers use different styles, such as starting figures at 10.

305B. It Is Part of a Compound Adjective.

a *five-day* week, a *three-month-old* baby, a *two-bedroom* apartment

305C. It Is a Fraction Without a Whole Number.

one-tenth of the voters; *three-fourths* full

But use figures when a whole number precedes: Add 1¾ cups of milk.

305D. It Begins a Sentence.

Three hundred eighty-six votes decided the election.

Never begin a sentence with a figure. If the number is a long one, rewrite the sentence to place the number elsewhere: The election was decided by *1,288* votes. OR Only *1,288* votes decided the election.

For resources to help you master this section's topics, log in to www.mywritinglab.com and select Abbreviations and Numbers from the list of subtopics.

306. Use Figures for

306A. Any Number Needing Three or More Words If Written Out (unless it begins a sentence. See 305D.):

The company is hiring 230 new workers.

Use commas to separate every set of three digits (except in serial, account, and telephone numbers; addresses; years in dates; and page numbers). Count from the right or from the decimal point:

1,288 votes	*$2,383,949.96*
A.D. *1066*	*2569* Palm Grove Road

Write very large round numbers as follows:

two million   *23 million*   *4.2 trillion*

306B. Numbers in These Special Uses:

addresses; room numbers; telephone numbers; television and radio station numbers; chapter, page, and line numbers; serial numbers; decimals and percentages; route numbers; times; statistics; precise measurements:

June *10, 2011*	*276* Wolf Road	Room *217*
459-7245	chapter *7*	Route *66*
67.6	Channel *6*	*5:02* a.m.
8 percent	*82* for; *47* against	Packers *27*, Jets *20*
6 by *3.2* inches [but *six feet long*]		*98.6°*F

Cautions:

- Do not use *-st, -th* . . . after figures in dates:
  Wrong: June *15th*, 2013
  Right: June *15*, 2013 [but *the fifteenth of June*]
- In formal writing, do not use the form *6/15/13* for a date.
- In writing a time, use figures with *a.m.* and *p.m.* and when emphasizing an exact time. Generally, use words otherwise:

3 p.m.	at *9:45* tomorrow
from *2:30* to *3:00* p.m.	the *8:02* train
four o'clock	around *half past five*

> *Note:* The times *12 a.m.* and *12 p.m.* can be confusing; which is noon and which is midnight? Say *noon* or *midnight* instead (and give both days that *midnight* separates): *noon Sunday, midnight Sunday/Monday, midnight June 3/4.*

306C. Groups of Numbers in the Same Passage (do not mix words and figures):

The control group's scores were *196, 57, 122, 10,* and *43.*

307. Write Amounts of Money as Follows:

I earn *ninety-five* dollars a day. I earn *$95.50* a day.
I earn *$310* a week. I won *$40, $30,* and *$5* at the races.
She won *a million dollars.* She won *$6 million.*
She won *$6,889,346.*

308–309. Abbreviations

Abbreviations are intended mainly for limited spaces, such as signs, lists, and documentation. In ordinary sentence writing, avoid abbreviations except for those listed in 308.

308. In Ordinary Writing, Abbreviate

308A. Certain Titles Before Proper Names:
Mr., Mrs., Ms., Dr., St. (saint), Messrs. (plural of *Mr.*), *Mmes.* (plural of *Ms.* or *Mrs.*) . . . :

Mr. John Barry	*Mr.* Barry	*Ms.* Suzuki
Mmes. Suzuki and Mosley		*Messrs.* Barry and Zito
St. Francis	*Rev.* Jules Bell	*Hon.* Ida Ives

But write *Reverend* and *Honorable* in full if they follow *the:*

the Reverend Jules Bell   *the Honorable* Ida Ives

Abbreviate military and civil titles unless you use only the person's last name:

Lt. Col. Harvey Perritt	*Sen.* Matthew Clemens
Lieutenant Colonel Perritt	*Senator* Clemens

308B. Degrees and Certain Other Titles After Proper Names:
Sr. (senior), Jr., Esq., M.A., Ph.D. . . . :

Ramez Hourani, *Sr.,* visited Barbara Bauer, *D.D.S.*

308C. Certain Expressions Used with Numerals:
a.m., p.m., B.C., A.D., No. (number), $:

9:30 a.m.   A.D. 1054   325 *B.C.*   *No.* 97   *$37.50*

Do not use such abbreviations without a numeral:

Wrong: She arrived this *a.m.*
Right: She arrived this *morning.*

> *Note:* You may choose to write *B.C.E. (before the common era)* and *C.E. (common era)* instead of *B.C.* and *A.D.* (*A.D.* precedes the year; the others follow.) You may also choose to write any of these sets of initials without periods; whichever style you use, be consistent.

308D. Certain Latin Phrases:
i.e. (that is), viz. (namely), e.g. (for example), cf. (compare), etc. (and so forth), vs. (versus).

Publishers tend to discourage the use of these abbreviations in the text of formal writing; you will do better to write out the English equivalents unless space is restricted (as in notes). Never write *and etc.*; it is redundant.

308E. Certain Government Agencies and Other Well-Known Organizations
(usually without periods): *CIA, NASA, NAACP, ABC, IBM.* To be sure that your reader knows the meaning of such initials, give the full title at first mention, preferably followed by the initials in parentheses:

The *American Automobile Association (AAA)* is campaigning for more highway funds. . . . Officials of the *AAA* are optimistic.

For resources to help you master this section's topics, log in to www.mywritinglab.com and select Abbreviations and Numbers from the list of subtopics.

309. In Ordinary Writing, Do *Not* Abbreviate

309A. Names of States, Countries, Months, Days, or Holidays

> **Wrong:** *Calif.* had a flood last *Tues., Xmas* Eve.
> **Right:** *California* had a flood last *Tuesday, Christmas* Eve.

309B. Personal Names

> *George* [not *Geo.*] Washington slept here.

309C. The Words *street, avenue, road, park,* **and** *company,* especially as part of proper names:

> **Wrong:** The Brady *Co.* is located on Park *Rd.*
> **Right:** The Brady *Company* is located on Park *Road.*

309D. The Word *and,* except in names of firms and in American Psychological Association (APA) references-list entries:

> Ways *and* Means Committee
> Brooks *&* Logan Corporation

> See 509B, pages 71–74, for APA style.

309E. References to a School Subject

> **Wrong:** The new *psych.* class is filled.
> **Right:** The new *psychology* class is filled.

309F. The Words *volume, chapter,* **and** *page,* except in documentation (see 509, pages 70–74), tabulations, and some technical writing.

310–314. Spelling

To your reader, misspellings are the most obvious of writing errors—like gravy stains on your best shirt or blouse. Yet they are easy for you, the writer, to miss. Do not rely on computer spelling checkers; most cannot distinguish between *from* and *form* or *there* and *their.* Rely on (1) **checking** a reputable dictionary when you are not sure, and (2) **proofreading** very carefully—more than just once or twice (see 506B, page 65).

310. Spelling Improvement Techniques

310A. Visualize the Correct Spelling of a Word. Look attentively at a word; then look away from it and try to see the printed word in your mind.

310B. Practice Pronouncing and Writing Troublesome Words. Say each word aloud, syllable by syllable, a number of times:

ath-let-ic	quan-ti-ty	gov-ern-ment
ac-ci-den-tal-ly	di-sas-trous	e-quip-ment
val-u-a-ble	tem-per-a-ture	min-i-a-ture

Practice writing each word several times. Keep a corrected list of your misspelled words.

310C. Distinguish Between Words Similar in Sound or Spelling. See 404, pages 54–59, for explanations of the following and many other such distinctions: *to/too/two, their/there/they're, its/it's, your/you're, loose/lose, whose/who's, affect/effect, accept/except.*

310D. Think of Related Words. Often, you can determine whether to end a word with *-er* or *-ar, -ence* or *-ance, -able* or *-ible,* and so forth, by thinking of a related form of the word in which the vowel is clearly pronounced.

For example, if you think of *definition,* you can be fairly sure that *definite* ends in *-ite.* Examine these pairs:

familiarity	familiar	stimulation	stimulant
grammatical	grammar	audition	audible
peculiarity	peculiar	symbolic	symbol
regularity	regular	confidential	confident
imagination	imaginary	existential	existence
desperation	desperate	dispensation	dispensable

Exception: sensation—sensible, sensitive

310E. Create and Use Memory Devices. Associate one word with another, find a word within a word, or make up jingles or nonsense sentences; such **mnemonics** can help you over the trouble spots in your problem words. Here are some examples:

> **Emma** is in a *dilemma.*
> She **dent**ed the *superinten**dent**'s* car.
> *Station**ery*** is pap**er.**
> A *princi**ple*** is a ru**le.**
> I want a *pie**ce*** of **pie.**
> I do not *bel**ie**ve* your **lie.**
> Poor *gram**mar*** will **mar** your writing.
> It is **vile** to have no *privi**le**ges.*
> The ***villa**in* owns a **villa in** Spain.
> There is **a rat** in *sepa**rat**e* and in *compa**rat**ive.*
> There is **iron** in the *env**iron**ment.*
> There is a **meter** in the *ce**meter**y.*
> **Tim** has a great *op**tim**ism.*
> With any *pro**f**essor,* one ***F*** is enough.

Mentally group words with similar characteristics, such as two sets of double letters (*accommodate, embarrass, possess*) or three *i*'s (*optimistic, primitive*) or names of occupations (*author, censor, conductor, emperor, investor, sponsor, professor*) or the three *-ceed* words: *proceed, exceed, succeed* (all other words ending in the same sound are spelled with *-cede: recede, concede, intercede* . . .; one exception: *supersede*).

311. The Five Basic Rules

311A. The *ie* **Rule.** You probably know the old jingle:

> Put *i* before *e* except after *c,*
> Or when sounded like *a,* as in *neighbor* and *weigh.*

That is, normally use *ie:*

ach**ie**ve	f**ie**ld	n**ie**ce
bel**ie**ve	gr**ie**f	rel**ie**ve
ch**ie**f	hyg**ie**ne	y**ie**ld
fr**ie**nd	misch**ie**f	misch**ie**vous

But after *c*, use *ei*:

ceiling	deceive	receive
conceive	perceive	receipt

Use *ei* also when the two letters sound like *AY*:

neighbor	weigh	freight
vein	sleigh	heir

Exceptions to the *ie* rule:

After *c*: *financier, society, species*

Other: *protein, seize, weird, counterfeit, forfeit, foreign, height, neither, leisure*

311B. The Final-*e* Rule. Drop a final silent *e* before a suffix beginning with a vowel (*a, e, i, o, u,* and here, *y*):

write + **ing** = writing	hope + **ed** = hoped
come + **ing** = coming	fame + **ous** = famous
love + **able** = lovable	scare + **y** = scary

Exception: *mileage*

But keep the *e*

After *c* and *g to keep a soft sound before a suffix beginning with *a* or *o*: *notice/able, change/able, trace/able, courage/ous, outrage/ous, venge/ance.*

To avoid confusion with other words: *singe + ing = singe/ing* (to avoid confusion with *singing*); *dye + ing = dye/ing.*

Be sure to keep the *e* when the suffix does not begin with a vowel: *hope/ful, love/less, lone/ly, safe/ty, state/ment, same/ness.* Exceptions: *judgment, argument, acknowledgment, truly, duly.*

311C. The Final-*y* Rule

Change a final *y* to *i* before any suffix—

happy + ness = happiness	cry + ed = cried
busy + ly = busily	lady + es = ladies

—unless the suffix begins with *i*—

cry/ing	bury/ing	try/ing	baby/ish

—or a vowel precedes the *y*:

chimn**ey**/s	ann**oy**/ed	monk**ey**/s

Exceptions: *lay, laid; pay, paid; say, said.*

311D. The Doubling Rule. This rule covers words ending in consonant-vowel-consonant (CVC), such as ***stop, refer.***

Double the final consonant before a suffix beginning with a vowel (including *y*):

cvc	cvc	cvc
drop, drop/**p**ing	bat, bat/**t**er	hum, hum/**m**able

If the original word has more than one syllable, double when the last syllable is accented:

cvc	cvc	cvc
oc**CUR**	oc**CUR**/red	oc**CUR**/rence

cvc	cvc	cvc
re**FER**	re**FER**/red	re**FER**/ral

cvc	cvc	cvc
be**GIN**	be**GIN**/**n**ing	be**GIN**/**n**er

Otherwise, do not double:

Not cvc: droop/ing (vvc), preVAIL/ing (vvc), dent/ed (vcc)

Not accented on last syllable: OFFer/ing, BENefit/ed, RECKon/ing

> *Note:* If the accent jumps back to an earlier syllable when the suffix is added, do not double: *conFER, CONfer/ence; reFER, REFer/ence.*

311E. The Let-It-Alone Rule. When adding prefixes or suffixes or combining roots, do not add or drop letters unless you know that one of the spelling rules applies or that the word is irregular (see 314):

Prefix + Root	Root + Suffix	Root + Root
dis/appear	careful/ly	book/keeper
dis/satisfied	immediate/ly	grand/daughter
mis/spell	comical/ly	
re/commend	state/ment	
un/necessary	achieve/ment	

312. Forming Plurals. To form most plurals, add *-s* to the singular (*toy, toys*; *dollar, dollars*; Lou *Lizak,* the *Lizaks*). The following generalizations cover most other plurals. Consult your dictionary in other cases or when in doubt.

312A. Add *-es* If You Hear an Added Syllable when you say a plural: *bush, bush/es*; *fox, fox/es*; *buzz, buzz/es*; *church, church/es*; *class, class/es.*

312B. Add *-es* When the Final-*y* Rule Applies (see 311C): *sky, skies*; *liberty, liberties*; *penny; pennies*; *fly, flies*; *lady, ladies.*

312C. Change Final *f* or *fe* to *v* and Add *-es* in the following and a few similar nouns: *calf, calves*; *knife, knives*; *wife, wives*; *loaf, loaves*; *wharf, wharves*; *half, halves*; *life, lives*; *shelf, shelves*; *wolf, wolves.*

312D. Add *-es* to Certain Nouns Ending in *o*.

tomato, tomato**es**; potato, potato**es**; hero, hero**es**

With musical terms, with words having a vowel before the *o*, and with most other singular nouns ending in *o*, add just *-s*:

solo, solos	piano, pianos	alto, altos
radio, radios	studio, studios	rodeo, rodeos

With some words, you may use either *-s* or *-es:*

> domino, domino**s**, domino**es**   zero, zero**s**, zero**es**

Consult a dictionary for other final-*o* word plurals.

312E. Change Final *-is* to *-es* in Many Words.

> basis, bas**es**; synopsis, synops**es**; oasis, oas**es**;
> hypothesis, hypothes**es**; thesis, thes**es**; axis, ax**es**;
> parenthesis, parenthes**es**; analysis, analys**es**; crisis, cris**es**;
> prosthesis, prosthes**es**

312F. Make Compound Words Plural as Follows: With solid
(unhyphenated) compounds, add the *-s* to the very end:
cupfuls, mouthfuls. With hyphenated compounds, add the *-s*
to the noun: *fathers-in-law, passers-by, senators-elect.*

**312G. Use the Foreign Plural for Some Nouns of Foreign
Origin:** *alumnus* (male), *alumni* (male or including both
sexes); *alumna, alumnae* (female); *stimulus, stimuli; stra-
tum, strata; curriculum, curricula.*

With many other such nouns, you may use either the foreign or English plural:

> radius, radi**i** or radius**es**; stadium, stadi**a** or stadium**s**;
> octopus, octop**i** or octopus**es**; index, indi**ces**
> or index**es**; appendix, append**ices** or appendix**es**;
> antenna, antenn**ae** [of insects] or antenna**s**
> [of electronic devices]; phenomenon, phenomen**a**
> or phenomenon**s**; criterion, criteri**a** or criterion**s**;
> vertebra, vertebr**ae** or vertebra**s**

Many of these use the foreign plural in scholarly or technical writing and the English plural in general writing.
Your dictionary may specify when each should be used.

> *Note:* Remember that *criteria, phenomena,* and *media* are
> plurals and require plural verbs. Most authorities also consider
> *data* plural in formal English; for the singular, use *body of
> data,* or, if appropriate, *database.*

312H. For Clarity, Use -'s for Plurals of Letters and Symbols.

> *Optimistic* has three *i'***s**. [not *three is*]

See 212B, page 37.

313. Nonstandard and Alternative Spellings

313A. Avoid Nonstandard Spellings, such as *nite, lite, rite*
(for *right*), and *thru,* which occur mostly in product
names. Do not use them elsewhere.

313B. Use Preferred Spellings. Some words have more than
one correct spelling: *programmer, programer; kidnapper,
kidnaper; dialogue, dialog; catalogue, catalog.* When the
dictionary lists two or more spellings, you are safer using
the first, which is considered preferred. In U.S. writing,
avoid British spellings, such as *colour, centre.*

314. One Hundred Problem Words. Many bother-
some spelling words have been explained in sections
310–313. Others—pairs of look-alikes or sound-alikes,
such as *advice* and *advise*— are clarified in 404, pages
54–59. Here are one hundred more "demons"; examine
them closely.

absence	excellent	personally
acknowledge	fascinating	playwright
acquaintance	fictitious	prejudice
acquire	forty	prevalent
across	fulfill	primitive
adolescence	guarantee	procedure
all right	guidance	psychology
amateur	hindrance	pursue
analysis	hypocrisy	questionnaire
apologize	incidentally	reminisce
apparent	independent	repetition
approximately	irrelevant	restaurant
article	irresistible	rhythm
auxiliary	knowledge	ridiculous
business	laboratory	sacrifice
calendar	maintenance	schedule
category	management	secretary
character	maneuver	sincerely
committee	mathematics	sophomore
competent	meant	souvenir
condemn	necessary	supposed to
conscientious	ninety	suppression
conscious	ninth	surprise
courteous	nucleus	synonym
criticism	occasionally	tendency
criticize	omission	tragedy
curiosity	opinion	twelfth
definite	opportunity	unusually
description	parallel	used to
develop	particularly	vacuum
discipline	perform	
doesn't	permanent	
eighth	permissible	
erroneous	perseverance	
exaggerate	persistent	

*For resources to help you master this section's topics,
log in to www.mywritinglab.com and select Spelling
from the list of subtopics.*

Following the rules for grammar, sentences, and mechanics is just the beginning of good writing. The clarity, style, and tone of your writing, and its consequent impression on your readers, depend largely on your choice of words.

401. Conciseness, Clarity, and Originality

A large vocabulary is an asset, but trying to impress with big words can actually weaken your writing. To convey your meaning accurately, clearly, concisely, and with originality, aim not for the biggest but for the best words.

401A. Be Concise.

Cut redundancies and other unneeded words. Redundancy means needless repetition, such as *six a.m. in the morning. Morning* and *a.m.* mean the same; say either, not both.

> *Much too wordy:* As I undertake this report, I would like to begin with the observation that the introductory section of the book on which I am reporting is too lengthy and should have been edited to make it more brief. In my opinion I think the author, in this excessively long introduction, discourages the reader from continuing further in the book.
>
> *Concise:* First, the book's introduction is too long, discouraging further reading.

Caution: Not all repetition is redundancy. Sometimes you must repeat for clarity or emphasis. See 503C, page 61.

Proofread carefully to catch double negatives, double subjects, and double *that*s. | ESL |

> Elmo would never have done ~~nothing~~ ^{anything} like that.
>
> They had~~n't~~ hardly enough food for survival. [*Hardly, barely,* and *scarcely* mean "almost not" and thus act as negatives.]
>
> After the trial the lawyer ~~she~~ congratulated us.
>
> The editorial claimed that, despite the nationwide decrease in crime, ~~that~~ our city was unsafe.

Two or more negatives in a sentence, even when technically correct, can confuse your reader. Most of the time it is better to state things positively:

> *Confusing:* The court has overturned the ruling that rescinded the ban on prohibiting street demonstrations.
>
> *Clear:* The court has ruled that street demonstrations are legal.

Trim overblown and indirect diction. Use plain, direct wording. It is generally clearer and carries more force than elaborate language. Avoid filling your writing with words ending in *-ion, -ity, -ment,* or *-ize,* such as *situation, activity, implement,* or *utilize.*

State your real subject and verb (the doer of the action, and the action itself) simply and directly:

> *Indirect, wordy, less clear:* The dissemination of the description of the suspect by the *police* soon led to her *apprehension.*
>
> *Direct, clearer:* The *police caught* the suspect soon after spreading her description.

See also 128E, page 25, on reduction, and 128G, page 26, on eliminating sentence clutter.

Examples of inflated diction, with concise alternatives:

Inflated	Concise
as to whether	whether
make a decision	decide
underwent a conversion	converted
determine the veracity of	verify
attain the lunar surface	reach the moon
utilize the audible emergency warning system	sound the alarm
We would like to bring to your attention the fact that your monthly payment of $42.75 is now overdue by ten days. Please remit the above sum to the company without delay. In the event of your failure to comply with this notice, the company shall be forced to impose a penalty charge for late payment.	Your monthly payment of $42.75 is ten days late. Please remit it at once to avoid a lateness penalty.

Trim these common wordy expressions:

Redundant, Inflated, or Otherwise Wordy	Concise
absolutely perfect, **very** unique	perfect, unique. See 119D, page 14.
maintenance **activity**, precipitation **activity**	maintenance, rain
actual fact, true fact	fact
and etc.; car makers **such as** GM, Ford, Toyota, **etc.**	etc. (*alone*); car makers such as GM, Ford, and Toyota
Where is the car **at?**	Where is the car?
at this (that) point in time	now (then)
ATM machine (the *M = machine*), **MLB baseball** (the *B = baseball*), **PIN number** (the *N = number*)	ATM, MLB (*or* major league baseball), PIN
on a daily **basis;** on the **basis** of this report	daily; from this report
but yet, but however	*use only one:* but *or* yet *or* however
each and every	*use only one:* each *or* every
end result	(*usually*) result
in the **event that**	if
residential **facility**	residential building, residence, home
the **fact that** she had no cash; **due to the fact that** he knew; **except for the fact that** it was void	her lack of cash; because he knew; except that it was void

Redundant, Inflated, or Otherwise Wordy	*Concise*
take the rainfall **factor** into consideration	consider rainfall
foreseeable future	future
It was a **free gift.**	It was free. OR It was a gift.
general consensus of opinion	consensus
generally always, usually always	*use only one:* always *or* generally *or* usually
that **kind** (*or* **sort**) **of a** man	that kind (*or* sort) of man
acts of a hostile **nature**	hostile acts
jumped **off of** the wall	jumped off the wall
continue **on**	(*usually*) continue
Meet me **outside of** the house.	Meet me outside the house.
personally, I . . .	I . . .
the registration **procedure;** the education **process;** It's **in the process of** being torn down.	registration; education; It's being torn down.
for the **purpose of** studying	to study; for studying
The **reason** they died **was because** no help came.	They died because no help came.
They know the **reason why** he lied.	They know why he lied.
refer back to; **return back** to	refer to; return to
in (with) regard(s) to this matter	about (*or* concerning) this matter
round **in shape;** blue in **color;** 6'11" tall **in height**	round; blue; 6'11" tall
emergency **situation;** The crime **situation** is improving. My financial **situation** is very poor.	emergency; Crime is down. I have little money.
there are few people **who** need	few people need
connect **up;** road ends **up;** climb **up;** meet **up with**	connect; ends; climb; meet

Avoid exaggerated and needless modifiers. The Grand Canyon is awesome; your friend's new shoes are not. Using an adjective such as *awesome, amazing, fabulous, fantastic, tremendous, great, unbelievable, incredible, iconic, classic,* or *terrific* to describe something a cut or two above the ordinary dilutes that adjective's real meaning. Use more-realistic words, such as *outstanding, first-rate, delightful, exciting, attractive, talented, stylish, thrilling, distinctive, exceptional, praiseworthy.*

Cut adverbs such as *totally* or *absolutely* when unnecessary: The bus was ~~totally~~ jammed and ~~absolutely~~ stifling.

Do not use *literally* (meaning "actually, in reality") when you mean its opposite, *figuratively:*

> **Wrong:** The other team *literally killed* us in lacrosse yesterday.
> **Right:** The other team *trounced* [or some similar word] us in lacrosse yesterday.

401B. Be Specific. A **general** term covers a wide grouping; a **specific** term mentions one of that grouping:

General	*Specific*
disease	cholera
writing	*Romeo and Juliet*
science	microbiology
music	"America the Beautiful"

(Of course, there may be intermediate terms: writing → play → tragedy → *Romeo and Juliet.*)

General versus specific statements. Sometimes you must generalize, as in topic and summary sentences:

> The economy shows signs of improving. [No specific facts are given.]

But to avoid vagueness and prove your point, you need sentences with specifics to support your generalization:

> This month new housing starts have risen 4.6 percent, and unemployment claims have dropped by 230,000.

Be as specific as your context allows: an *orange-streaked* (not just *beautiful*) sunset; *two dozen* (not *many*) onlookers; her *dazzling whirls and leaps* (not her *fine dancing*).

General or Vague	*More Specific*
many, a number of, some, a lot of	more than 150, about forty thousand, fewer than twenty, nearly half . . .
thing	item, detail, article, idea, deed, quality, event, incident, point (*for* thing she said), foods (*for* things to eat), sights (*for* things to see) . . .
stuff	goods, items, equipment, material(s), books, groceries . . .
fine, nice, wonderful, great	sunny, friendly, considerate, record-setting, inspiring . . .

For another example, compare paragraphs 4A and 4B in section 503B, page 61.

401C. Consider Connotation. *Thrifty, frugal, stingy,* and *parsimonious* all refer to holding on to one's money, but each word has a different **connotation,** or implied meaning: you convey a negative rather than a positive connotation if you use *parsimonious* instead of *thrifty.* Likewise, *avoid* and *evade* have different implications, as do *decline* and *refuse.* A good dictionary will explain shades of difference among similar words.

401D. Use Fresh, Original Wording **Avoid clichés** (klee SHAYZ)—trite, overused expressions, such as *last but not least,* which bore readers and signal your lack of originality. Be suspicious of expressions that pop too readily into your mind—they may well be clichés.

Some Clichés as Old as the Hills

add insult to injury	my mind was a blank
all in a day's work	quick as a wink
better late than never	rags to riches
between a rock and	raining cats and dogs
a hard place	sick as a dog
down but not out	soft as silk
easier said than done	start from scratch
first and foremost	time flew by
few and far between	tip of the iceberg
hungry as a horse	tried and true
in this day and age	water under the bridge
left no stone unturned	work like a dog

Avoid overusing the same words. Watch for words you tend to use too often, such as *very* (try *quite, rather,* or *extremely;* or better, specify a degree: not *very cold* but *so cold that our eyelids froze*). Another greatly overused word is *get* (or *got*). See 402C.

Use imaginative language. For originality, use your own imaginative comparisons—**metaphors** or **similes** (SIM uh leez)—where appropriate:

> **Metaphor:** Waking in her dark apartment, she could see, all around her, tiny green lights—from the computer modem, the smoke alarm, the microwave, the cable box, the wall phone—*silent sentinels of her electronic army.*
>
> **Simile** (uses *like* or *as*): . . . **like** *silent sentinels of her electronic army.*

402. Standard, Appropriate English

Standard English is writing or speaking that is both grammatical and universally understood. It can range from fully **formal**—such as *One must choose wisely with whom one associates*—to quite **informal,** or **colloquial**—such as *Use your head when you pick your pals.*

Nonstandard English contains expressions and usages that are outside the conventions of standard English—such as *I ain't got no money* or *You be on the right road.* Varieties of nonstandard English may include different slang or dialect words (see 402B). Though certain nonstandard conventions may be acceptable among some groups, standard English is the norm for communication throughout the English-speaking world.

402A. Formal Versus Informal. Within standard English, there is no sharp borderline between formal and informal; think of *very formal* and *very informal* as the top and bottom rungs of a ladder, with a number of rungs between them. Keep your language level consistent—on the same rung—within each piece of writing.

Determine the best rung for each piece you write, from

- Its **nature** (a technical report, a campus paper editorial, a humorous essay . . .)
- Its **purpose** (to amuse, to stimulate thought . . .)

- Its **occasion** (a sports victory, a eulogy . . .)
- Its intended **audience** (high school alumni, a college acceptance committee . . .)

A research paper or an article for a scholarly journal, for example, would use the top, most formal rung; a light essay or a talk at a student club meeting would use a less formal rung. Some good aids to language levels are *The New Fowler's Modern English Usage* (3rd ed.) and the *Harper Dictionary of Contemporary Usage* (2nd ed.). But your best aid is to read (and listen) extensively on various levels.

In most formal writing, avoid the following: contractions (*you're, we've*), shortened word forms (*math* for *mathematics*), and the use of *you* for *a person* (*in ancient Rome, when* you *met . . .*).

402B. Limited-Circulation Words. Unless you are representing the speech of a certain group, do not use words of types not universally understood. These types include

> **Slang** (words such as *dude* [currently, *a man,* of almost any kind], *bling* [*flashy ornamentation*], or *zone out* [*lose all concentration*]). Slang expressions are generally short-lived, arising among a particular social group, such as teenagers—though the electronic media may widen their circulation.
>
> **Regionalisms or dialect words** (words known only within certain geographical areas or population groups—such as *tonic* or *pop* for *flavored soda water,* or *sack* for *paper bag*).
>
> **Jargon** (technical or other vocabulary known only to a particular group): *hemodynamically optimal pacing site* is medical jargon; *sack* is baseball jargon for *a base* but football jargon for *tackling the quarterback.* If you must use a word unknown to most general readers, define it in parentheses following its first use—the way *jargon* is defined just above.
>
> **Email and text-messaging shortcuts,** such as *BRB* (*be right back*) or *IMHO* (*in my humble opinion*), and emoticons such as :-) for a smile. See 504, page 63.

402C. Some Common Expressions to Avoid. In standard English, never use the boldfaced words labeled *ungrammatical* in the list below. Mostly avoid the other boldfaced expressions as well; follow the principles you have learned in 402A and B.

> red **and/or** green (legal and business jargon, also sometimes unclear). Say *red or green or both.*
>
> **anyways, anywheres, everywheres, nowheres, somewheres** (ungrammatical). Say *anyway* or *any way, anywhere, everywhere.* . . .
>
> **aren't I** (ungrammatical). Say *am I not.*
>
> **awful.** Say *quite bad, ugly, shocking.* . . .
>
> **awful(ly)** good. Say *quite, very, extremely.*
>
> want it **badly.** Say *greatly, urgently.* . . .
>
> **being as (how), being that.** Say *because, since.*
>
> You **better** do it. Say *You had better, You'd better.*
>
> between **you and I,** told **him and I . . .** (ungrammatical). After a preposition or action verb, say *you and me, him and me.* See 122C, page 17.

a **bunch** of people. Say *group, crowd.*

I **bust (busted, bursted)** the balloons (ungrammatical). Say *I burst the balloons* (present and past), *I have burst the balloons.*

He had no doubt **but that (but what)** she knew it. Say *He had no doubt that.*

can't hardly (scarcely, barely) (ungrammatical). Say *can hardly, scarcely, barely.* See 401A, page 50.

can't help but love you. Say *can't help loving you.*

Contact me tomorrow (business jargon). Say *Call, See, Email.* . . . (Some authorities, however, do accept the verb *contact* in formal usage, to mean "get in touch with.") *Contact* as a noun is always acceptable: *Divers made contact with the wreck.*

cop(s). Say *police officer(s), police.*

could of, may of, might of, must of, ought to of, should of, would of (ungrammatical). Say *could have, may have, might have* . . . or, informally, *could've, may've, might've.* . . .

a couple (of) friends, days, problems. . . . Say *two friends, three days, several problems.* . . . Save *couple* for a joined pair, such as *an engaged couple.*

Due to the time, we left. Say *Because of the time.* (*Due to* is acceptable after *be* or *seem: The delay was due to rain.*) See *fact that,* 401A, page 50.

He **enthused (was enthused)** about it. Say *He was enthusiastic about it.*

reading Updike, Bellow, **etc.** In sentence writing, say *and others* or *and so forth,* or say *reading writers such as Updike and Bellow.*

every bit as old as. Say *just as old as.*

every so often, every once in a while. Say *occasionally, from time to time.*

every which way. Say *every way.*

She has a **funny** accent. Say *peculiar, odd.*

get there, **get** away, (have) **got** to, **get** ready, **got** married, **get** tired. . . . Do not overuse *get* and *got.* Say *arrive, escape, must* or *have to, prepare, (were) married, grow tired.* . . . See *have got* below.

gonna, gotta, wanna, oughta, shoulda. . . . Careless speech for *going to, have to, want to, ought to, should have.* . . . Never write such words (unless reproducing careless speech in dialogue).

If I **had of** known (ungrammatical). Say *had known.*

He **had(n't) ought to** go (ungrammatical). Say *He ought to go, he ought not (to) go.*

a half a page. Say *a half page, half a page.*

They **have got** the answer. Say *have the answer.*

hisself, ourself(s), yourselfs, themself(s), theirself(s), theirselves (ungrammatical). Say *himself, ourselves, yourselves, themselves.*

Hopefully, the bus will arrive soon. Conservative authorities shun such usage as illogical, because *hopefully* means "full of hope" (the bus is not full of hope). The logical usage is *We hope the bus will arrive soon.* (More-liberal authorities accept *hopefully* as a sentence adverb, like *frankly* or *seriously.*)

if and when I go. Generally, say either *if I go* or *when I go.*

Ellington's music **impacted (on)** three generations (business-technical jargon). Say *greatly affected, influenced, brought happiness to.* . . . *Impact* as a noun (*a great impact*) is acceptable.

irregardless (illogical prefix). Say *regardless.*

is when, is where. See 130E, page 29.

It being late, we left. Say *Because it was late* or *Since it was late.* See 129A, page 26, on *it being* in fragments.

kid(s). Say *child(ren).*

kind of (sort of) soft. Say *rather soft, somewhat soft,* or just *soft.*

a lot (often misspelled *alot*) **of, lots of.** Say *much, many;* better, specify: *fifty* or *dozens of.* See 401B, page 51.

mad at you. Say *angry with you. Mad* means "insane."

most all the books. Say *almost all.*

nowhere near ready. Say *not nearly ready.*

O.K., OK, okay. Say *all right, correct* (adj.); *approval* (noun); *approve* (verb).

everyone **outside of** John. Say *except John.*

plan on going. Say *plan to go.*

plenty good. Say *quite good.* (*Plenty* is acceptable as a noun: *plenty of fish.*)

You can have money **plus** fun. You can arrive early; **plus,** you can stay late (mostly business-commercial jargon). Reserve *plus* mostly for adddition; avoid it in other formal writing. Say *You can have [both] money and fun. You can arrive early; besides [or also, moreover], you can stay late.*

a **pretty** sum; a **pretty** long ride. Say *quite a large sum, a fairly long ride.* . . .

real good, **real** smooth. Say *very, quite, remarkably.* . . .

He looked **really** old. Say *quite old, aged.*

They were **right** tired (regionalism). They went **right** home. Say *quite tired, directly home.*

seeing as how, seeing that. Say *since, because.*

It **seldom ever** changed. Say *seldom or never, seldom if ever, hardly ever.*

in bad **shape.** Say *in poor condition.*

They were **so** happy. Say *They were so happy that they wept.* See 130C, page 29.

She ran **so** she could stay fit. Say *so that she could.* . . .

The bill was vague, **so** the President vetoed it. Joining too many independent clauses with *so* gives your writing a too-casual tone. Recast the sentence: *The President vetoed the bill because it was vague.*

James is **some** player! He worried **some.** Say *James is quite a player! He worried somewhat* or *a little.*

It was **such** a loud noise. There is **no such a** place. Say *such a loud noise that her ears hurt* [see 130C, page 29]. *There is no such place.*

This would **sure** help. Say *surely help.* See 119A, page 14.

terribly sad, a **terrific** win. Say *extremely sad, a last-minute win, an exciting win.*

them weapons (ungrammatical). Say *those weapons.*

these kind (sort, type), those kind (ungrammatical). Say *this kind, that kind, this sort, that type. Kind, type,* and *sort* are singular; they must take singular modifiers. For plurals, say *these kinds, those types.* . . .

this (these) here, that (those) there (ungrammatical). Say just *this, that, these, those.*

Try and win. Be **sure and** vote. Say *Try to win. Be sure to vote.*

It was **very** appreciated. Say *very much, greatly.*

She **waited on** a bus (regionalism). Say *waited for.* But *she waited on [served] the mayor's table* is correct.

Jones read in the newspaper **where** Smith had died. Say *that Smith had died.*

If Jackson **would have** retired, he **would have** kept his reputation (ungrammatical). Say *If Jackson had retired.* See 116G, page 11.

For resources to help you master this section's topics, log in to www.mywritinglab.com and select Standard and Non-Standard English from the list of subtopics.

403. Nondiscriminatory Terms

403A. Nonsexist Terms | ESL

Pronouns. Avoid using *he, his,* or *him* in contexts applicable to both sexes, as in *Every traveler needs **his** passport.* For nonsexist alternatives, review 121A, page 16.

Nouns. Where both sexes are or may be included, replace single-sex nouns with gender-neutral ones:

Single-sex	Inclusive
mankind	humankind
seaman	sailor
policeman	(police) officer
mailman	mail carrier
fireman	firefighter
repairman	repairer
salesman	salesperson
housewife	homemaker
waitress	server
stewardess	flight attendant
the average man	the average person

Do not mention the sex of a worker (e.g., *lady mechanic, woman pilot*) except where needed, as in *She was the first woman pilot in America.* Refer to females beyond high school age as (*young*) *women,* not *girls.* Avoid expressions that put women in a lower category, such as *farmers and their wives* (the wives work the farm too; say just *farmers* or *farm families*), *man and wife* (say *husband and wife*).

403B. Other Nondiscriminatory Terms

Ethnic, racial, religious. Avoid all ethnic stereotyping and terms associated with it, as well as negative terms such as *culturally deprived.* Avoid terms that place Europe at the center of the world (say *East Asian,* not *Far Eastern* [that is, far east of Europe] or *Oriental*) or that cast one race as dominant: *nonwhite* may imply that white is the racial standard; *flesh-colored*—meaning white flesh—ignores most of the world; words that equate black with bad (*a black mark, blacklist*) may suggest African racial inferiority.

Call racial, national, ethnic, and religious groups by the names they prefer: *African Americans, American Indians* (or *Native Americans*), *Inuit* (not *Eskimos*). Omit hyphens in terms such as *Italian American* and *Chinese American.*

Do not label a religion a *cult;* say *house of worship,* not *church* (unless referring specifically to Christians).

Disabilities. Say *disability* rather than *handicap* (a disability is not necessarily a handicap). Do not refer to persons with disabilities as *crippled, deformed, retarded, invalids, mental cases,* and the like; do not call those without disabilities *normal* (implying abnormality in those with disabilities).

Focus on the person, not the disability: identify a person not as *the paraplegic* or *the amputee* but as, for example, *the accountant who uses a wheelchair.*

404. Similar Words Often Confused

Below are sets of two (or more) words that may cause confusion because of their similar appearance, sound, spelling, or meaning. The most common troublemakers are in color.

a, an. See 120A, page 14.

accept, except. *Accept* (verb) means "to receive": Taylor Swift *accepted* the Grammy Award.

Except (usually preposition) means "excluding": He has read all Shakespeare's plays *except Cymbeline.*

Note: Except is occasionally a verb, meaning "to exclude": The judge told the lawyers to *except* the disputed testimony from their summations.

adapt, adopt. *Adapt* means "to adjust or make suitable": Immigrants often find it difficult to *adapt* their lives to American ways.

Adopt means "to take as one's own": The young aspiring actress *adopted* the mannerisms of her favorite film star. The couple *adopted* a girl.

advice (say *ad VICE*), **advise** (say *ad VIZE*). *Advice* (noun) means "counsel": I was skeptical of the salesperson's *advice.*

Advise (verb) means "to give advice": The salesperson *advised* me to buy the larger size.

affect, effect. Most commonly, *affect* (verb) means "to influence, to have an effect on": The mortgage crisis soon *affected* the stock market.

Most commonly, *effect* (noun) means "a result, consequence, outcome": The mortgage crisis had a disastrous *effect* on the stock market.

Note: Less commonly, *affect* (as a verb) means "to pretend or imitate": He *affected* a British accent. *Effect* (as a verb) means "to accomplish, to bring about": The medicine *effected* a cure.

afterward, afterwards. Americans prefer *afterward;* the British, *afterwards.*

aggravate, irritate. Do not use *aggravate* for *annoy* or *irritate,* as in His lateness *aggravates* me. *Aggravate* means "to worsen (an already existing condition)": Lifting the heavy bags *aggravated* the pain in her back.

Irritate means "to annoy": That loud, tinny music *irritates* me. *Irritate* also means "make sore, rough, or inflamed": This rough wool *irritates* my skin.

aisle, isle. An *aisle* is a passage between sections of seats: the side *aisle*.

An *isle* is an island: the Emerald *Isle*.

all ready, already. *All ready* means "completely ready": the runner was *all ready* for the marathon. It also refers to the readiness of every person or thing: The trucks were *all ready* to proceed [*all* the trucks were *ready* to proceed].

Already means "previously" or "by this time": Karl had *already* crossed the finish line.

all together, altogether. *All together* means "in or as a group": We were *all together* at the reunion.

Altogether means "wholly, completely, in all": His promotion was *altogether* unexpected. These purchases come to $46.87 *altogether*.

allusion, illusion, delusion. *Allusion* means "an indirect reference": The novel has many Shakespearean *allusions*.

Illusion means "a temporary false perception; a magic trick": It was an optical *illusion*.

Delusion refers to a lasting false perception or belief about oneself or other persons or things: He held the *delusion* that she had long been in love with him.

altar, alter. An *altar* is a table for religious services: The minister approached the *altar*.

To *alter* is to change: If it rains, we will have to *alter* our picnic plans.

among. See *between*.

amoral, immoral. *Amoral* means "not concerned with morality": An infant's acts are *amoral*.

Immoral means "against morality": Murder is *immoral*.

amount, number. *Amount* refers to things in bulk or mass: a large *amount* of grain; no *amount* of persuasion.

Number refers to countable things: a *number* of books, a *number* of reasons.

ante-, anti-. Both are prefixes. *Ante-* means "before": *anteroom, antedate, antecedent*.

Anti- means "against": *antibody, antisocial, antidote*.

anxious, eager. *Anxious* conveys worry or unease: Katie grew *anxious* when her ride to her big job interview was late.

Eager conveys strong desire: They were *eager* to marry.

any more, anymore. *Any more* means "additional": Is there *any more* fuel? There isn't *any more*.

Anymore means "at present" or "any longer": He doesn't write home *anymore*.

any one, anyone. *Any one* refers to any single item of a number of items: *Any one* of these buses will take you downtown.

Anyone means "any person, anybody": Does *anyone* want a ride downtown?

apt, likely, liable. *Apt* refers to probability based on normal, habitual, or customary tendency: He was *apt* to throw things when frustrated.

Likely indicates mere probability: It is *likely* to rain.

Liable, strictly, refers to legal responsibility: Jaywalkers are *liable* to arrest. Informally, it is used also with any

undesirable or undesired risk: He's *liable* to get into trouble.

as, like. See *like*.

awhile, a while. *Awhile* (adverb) cannot be the object (noun) of *for* or *in*. One may stay *awhile* (adverb), stay for a *while* (noun), stay a *while* (noun), but not stay for *awhile* (adverb).

bad, badly. See 119C, page 14.

beside, besides. *Beside* (preposition) means "at the side of": She stood *beside* me [at my side] throughout the ordeal.

Besides (preposition, conjunctive adverb) means "other than" or "in addition (to)": *Besides* me, only five students came. I was exasperated; *besides*, I was lonely.

between, among. *Between* implies *two* persons or things in a relationship; *among* implies *three or more*: Emissaries shuttled *between* London and Moscow. A dispute arose *among* the four nations.

You may use *between* with more than two if the relationships are between pairs in the group: Flights *between* New York, Milwaukee, and Detroit were delayed [between any two of the three].

born, borne. Use *born* (after *be*) only to mean "have one's birth": They *were born* [had their birth] in Brazil.

Use *borne* before *by* and elsewhere: The baby was *borne by* a surrogate mother. She has *borne* two sons. Zullo has *borne* the burdens of office well.

brake, break. *Brake* refers to stopping: Apply the *brake*. *Brake* the car carefully.

Break refers to destroying, damaging, exceeding, or interrupting: Don't *break* the glass. I'll *break* the record. Take a ten-minute *break*.

bring, take. In precise usage, *bring* means "to come (here) with" and *take* means "to go (there) with": *Take* this check to the bank and *bring* back the cash.

can, may. In formal usage, *can* means "to be able to" (They *can* solve any equation), and *may* means "to have permission to" (You *may* leave now). *May* also expresses possibility: It *may* snow tonight.

Speakers will often resort to *can* to avoid the ambiguity caused by the two meanings of *may*: *They may enter the country through Miami* means either (1) that they are undecided where to enter, or (2) that customs officials will permit them to enter there. *They can enter the country through Miami* clarifies the matter.

canvas, canvass. A *canvas* is a cloth: Buy a *canvas* tent. *Canvass* means "to solicit": *Canvass* the area for votes.

capitol, capital. Use *capitol* only for the building where a legislature meets: The governor's office is in the *Capitol*.

Elsewhere, use *capital*: Austin is the state *capital* [seat of government]. The firm has little *capital* [money]. It was a *capital* [first-rate] idea. Murder can be a *capital* offense [one punishable by death].

carat, karat, caret, carrot. Gems are weighted in *carats*, gold in *karats*. A *caret* (∧) signals an omission: I ∧ going home. A *carrot* is a vegetable.

casual, causal. *Casual* means "occurring by chance, informal, unplanned": Ours was just a *casual* meeting. Wear *casual* clothes.

Causal means "involving cause": No *causal* relationship was found between his drinking and his death.

censor, censure, censer. To *censor* is to examine written, visual, or other material to suppress what the *censor* (person censoring) considers objectionable: Many parents want to *censor* violent television shows. The dictator had his nation's press *censored* to suppress criticism of him.

To *censure* is to criticize or blame: The senator was *censured* for unethical conduct.

A *censer* is a container for the burning of incense.

cite, site, sight. *Cite* means "to quote an authority or give an example": Did you *cite* all your sources in your paper?

Site means "location": Here is the new building *site*.

Sight refers to seeing: The ship's lookout *sighted* land. Use your *sight* and hearing.

classic, classical. *Classic* means "of the highest class or quality": *Hamlet* is a *classic* play.

Classical means "pertaining to the art and life of ancient Greece and Rome": *Classical* Greek art idealized the human figure.

Classical music refers to symphonies and the like.

coarse, course. *Coarse* means "rough, not fine": *coarse* wool.

A *course* is a path or a series of lessons: race *course*, art *course*. Of *course* means "certainly."

compare to, compare with. *Compare to* means "to liken, to point out one or more similarities": The rookie is being *compared to* Ichiro Suzuki.

Compare with means "to examine to determine similarities and differences": The report *compares* students' S.A.T. scores *with* their college admission and graduation rates.

compliment, complement. *Compliment* means "to express praise": The manager *complimented* her workers for their efficiency.

Complement means "to complete, enhance, or bring to perfection": The illustrations should *complement* the text. The nouns *compliment* and *complement* are distinguished similarly. Free tickets are *complimentary*.

comprise, compose, include. *Comprise* means "to be made up of (in entirety)." The whole *comprises* the parts: Our league *comprises* eight teams. Do not use *is comprised of*.

Compose means "to make up, constitute." It is the opposite of *comprise*. The parts *compose* the whole: Eight teams *compose* our league. Our league *is composed of* eight teams.

Include means "to contain (but not necessarily in entirety)": Our league *includes* teams in Bennington and Manchester.

continual, continuous. *Continual* means "frequently repeated": She receives *continual* annoying calls from a man she dislikes.

Continuous means "without interruption": The *continuous* roar of the machinery annoyed Sam.

convince, persuade. Some authorities see these words as synonyms. Others say to use *convince* (followed by *of* or *that*—not by *to*) for changing a person's belief (Olga *convinced* me *that* she was right. *Convince* me *of* your sincerity), but to use *persuade* for moving a person to action (She *persuaded* me to go).

correspond to, correspond with. *Correspond to* means "to be similar or analogous to": The German gymnasium *corresponds to* the American preparatory school.

Correspond with means "to be in agreement or conformity with": His behavior did not *correspond with* our rules. It also means "to communicate with by exchange of letters."

council, counsel, consul. *Council* means "a deliberative assembly": The Parish *Council* debated the issue.

Counsel (noun) means "advice" or "attorney": He sought the *counsel* of a psychologist. She is the *counsel* for the defense. *Counsel* (verb) means "to advise": They *counseled* us to wait before marrying.

Consul means "an officer in the foreign service": The distinguished guest was the *consul* from Botswana.

credible, credulous, creditable. *Credible* means "believable": A witness's testimony must be *credible*.

Credulous means "too ready to believe; gullible": A *credulous* person is easily duped.

Creditable means "praiseworthy": The young pianist gave a *creditable* performance of a difficult work.

decent (say *DEE cent*), **descent** (say *de CENT*). *Decent* means "proper, moral, in good taste," or "adequate ": This is not a *decent* film for children. It was a *decent* but not an outstanding performance.

Descent means "a going down" or "ancestry": The plane's *descent* was bumpy. He's of Guyanese *descent*.

delusion. See *allusion*.

device (say *de VICE*), **devise** (say *de VIZE*). A *device* (noun) is an invention or a piece of equipment: This *device* opens the door remotely.

To *devise* (verb) is to invent: *Devise* a new mousetrap.

different from, different than. Formal usage requires *different from*: His paper is hardly *different from* yours.

> *Note:* Many authorities consider *different than* acceptable when introducing a clause: The results were *different than* we had expected [smoother than *different from what*].

differ from, differ with. *Differ from* expresses unlikeness: His paper *differs* greatly *from* mine.

Differ with expresses divergence of opinion: The President *differed with* Congress regarding health care.

disinterested, uninterested. *Disinterested* means "not influenced by personal interest; impartial, unbiased": A *disinterested* judge gives fair rulings.

Uninterested means simply "not interested": The *uninterested* judge dozed on the bench.

each other, one another. In formal usage, *each other* refers to two persons or things: The lovers gazed fondly at *each other*. *One another* refers to more than two: The jurors looked at *one another* with relief when the judge dismissed them all.

eager. See *anxious*.

effect. See *affect*.

emigrate, immigrate. *Emigrate* means "to leave a country"; *immigrate* means "to enter a new country": Millions *emigrated* from Europe. They *immigrated* to America.

eminent, imminent. *Eminent* means "distinguished": She's an *eminent* surgeon.

Imminent means "about to happen": Rain is *imminent*.

ensure, insure. *Ensure* is preferred for "make sure, guarantee": To *ensure* your safety, wear seat belts.

Insure refers to insurance (protection against loss): *Insure* your valuables.

envelop (say *en VELL up*)**, envelope** (say *EN vel ope* or *ON vel ope*). To *envelop* (verb) is to surround: Fog *envelops* us. An *envelope* (noun) holds a letter: Seal the *envelope*.

everyone, every one. *Everyone* means "everybody": *Everyone* [everybody] left early.

Elsewhere, use *every one* (meaning "every single item or person"): *Every one* of the questions was hard. I could answer *every one*. *Every one* of the applicants was interviewed.

except. See *accept*.

famous, notable, notorious. *Famous* means "widely known"; it usually has favorable connotations.

Notable means "worthy of note" or "prominent"; a person can be *notable* without being *famous*.

Notorious means "widely known in an unfavorable way": Al Capone was a *notorious* gangster.

farther, further. *Farther* refers to physical distance: The gasoline station is *farther* away than I thought.

Further means "to a greater extent or degree": The UN decided to discuss the issue *further*.

fewer, less. *Fewer* refers to number; use it with countable things: This paper has *fewer* errors than your last one.

Use *less* with things that are not countable but are considered in bulk or mass: *Less* snow fell this year.

formally, formerly. *Formally* means "according to proper form": Introduce us *formally*.

Formerly means "previously": They *formerly* lived on a farm.

former, latter; first, last. *Former* and *latter* refer to the first and second named of only two items: Concerning jazz and rock, she prefers the *former* [jazz], but he prefers the *latter* [rock]. In a series of three or more, use *first* and *last*.

Often, however, your sentence will read better without *former* or *latter*: In popular music she prefers jazz, though he prefers rock.

forth, fourth. *Forth* means "forward": Go *forth* and conquer. *Fourth* is 4th: They paraded on the *Fourth* of July.

good, well. See 119C, page 14.

hanged, hung. Strict usage requires *hanged* when you mean "executed": She was *hanged* as a spy.

Elsewhere, use *hung*. They *hung* the flag high.

healthy, healthful. *Healthy* means "possessing health": The children are *healthy*.

Healthful means "conducive to health": Bran is *healthful*.

historic, historical. *Historic* means "famous or important in history": July 4, 1776, is a *historic* date.

Historical means "pertaining to history": Good *historical* novels immerse us in their times.

if, whether. When presenting alternatives, preferably use *whether* for precision: Tell us *whether* (not *if*) you pass or fail. Also, drop an unneeded *or not* after *whether*: He was unsure *whether* or not to go.

illusion. See *allusion*.

immigrate. See *emigrate*.

imminent. See *eminent*.

immoral. See *amoral*.

imply, infer. Writers or speakers *imply* (state indirectly or suggest): The instructor's tone of voice *implied* that she would mark our papers strictly.

Readers or listeners *infer* (draw a conclusion or derive by reasoning): From the instructor's tone of voice we *inferred* that she would mark our papers strictly.

in, into. Use *into* with movement from outside to inside: The nurse ran *into* Wilcox's room.

Elsewhere, use *in*: Wilcox lay quietly *in* his bed.

include. See *comprise*.

incredible, incredulous. A fact or happening is *incredible* (unbelievable): Astronomical distances are *incredible*.

A person is *incredulous* (unbelieving): He was *incredulous* when told how far the universe extends.

individual, person, party. Do not use *party* or *individual* when you mean simply *person*: They heard from a certain *person* (not *individual* or *party*) that she was engaged. Except in legal usage, and when you mean "one taking part," do not use *party* to refer to one person.

Use *individual* only when emphasizing a person's singleness: Will you act with the group or as an *individual*?

ingenious (say *in JEEN yus*)**, ingenuous** (say *in JENN yu us*). *Ingenious* means "clever"; *ingenuous* means "naive, having childlike frankness": *Ingenious* swindlers forged a deed to the Brooklyn Bridge and sold it to an *ingenuous* out-of-towner.

instance, instants, instant's. *Instance* means "a case or example": She remembered each *instance* of his kindness. [plural: *instances*]

Instants is the plural of *instant*, which means "a brief time, a particular moment": She did it in a few *instants*.

Instant's is the possessive of *instant*: The officer responded at an *instant's* notice.

insure. See *ensure*.

irritate. See *aggravate*.

isle. See *aisle*.

its, it's. *Its* is the possessive of *it*: The dog bared *its* teeth.

It's is the contraction of *it is*. Use *it's* only if you can correctly substitute *it is* in your sentence: *It's* [it is] a friendly dog.

See 122F, page 18.

last, latter. See *former*.

later, latter. *Later*, the comparative from of *late*, means "more late." For *latter*, see *former*.

lay. See *lie*.

lead, led. *Lead* (rhymes with *need*) is the present tense of the verb meaning "to conduct, to be or go at the head of, to show the way": Jenks will *lead* the scout troop. *Lead* me to the food.

Led is the past tense and past participle of the same verb: Jenks [*has*] *led* the troop for two years.

Lead (rhymes with *dead*) is a metal: I need a *lead* pipe.

learn, teach. *Learn* means "to acquire knowledge": Toddlers must *learn* not to touch electrical outlets.

Teach means "to impart knowledge": Parents must *teach* toddlers not to touch electrical outlets.

leave, let. *Leave* means "to depart": I must *leave* now.

Let means "to permit": *Let* me go.

lend, loan. In formal usage, avoid *loan* as a verb. Use *lend, lent, lent*: Bernie *lent* [not *loaned*] me his car.

Loan is properly a noun: He took out a *loan*.

less. See *fewer*.

lessen, lesson. To *lessen* is to diminish, decrease: Her ardor for him *lessened* as she discovered his slovenly habits. The antibiotics *lessened* his pain.

A *lesson* is a unit of learning: Study your *lesson*.

liable, likely. See *apt*.

lie, lay. *Lie* means "to rest" and is an intransitive verb (it never takes an object): Don't *lie* on the new couch. The islands *lie* under the tropical sun. Here *lies* Jeremiah Todd.

Lay means "to put, to place" and is a transitive verb (it must take an object): *Lay* your *head* on this pillow. Let me *lay* your *fears* to rest.

To complicate matters, the past tense of *lie* is spelled and pronounced the same as the present tense of *lay*:

Present	**Past**	**Past Participle**
lie [rest] →	lay [rested] →	(has) lain [rested]
lay [place] →	laid [placed] →	(has) laid [placed]

Yesterday Sandra *lay* [*rested*] too long in the sun. She should not have *lain* [*rested*] there so long. Yesterday the workers *laid* [*placed*] the foundation. They have *laid* [*placed*] it quickly.

like, as. Although you may often see *like* (preposition) in place of *as* (conjunction), stay away from such usage. Reject *like* wherever *as*, *as if*, or *as though* sounds right: The old house had remained just *as* (not *like*) I remembered it. It happened just *as* (not *like*) [it did] in the novel. Act *as if* (or *as though*, but not *like*) you belong here. He looks *as though* he needs help.

The way is a good alternative: The old house had remained just *the way* I remembered it.

loan. See *lend*.

loose, lose. *Loose* (usually adjective—rhymes with *goose*) is the opposite of *tight* or *confined*: The *loose* knot came undone. The lions are *loose*! *Loose* is also sometimes a verb: Nero *loosed* the lions on them.

Lose (verb—rhymes with *snooze*) is the opposite of *find* or *win*: Did you *lose* your keys? We may *lose* the game.

may. See *can*.

maybe, may be. *Maybe* is an adverb meaning "perhaps": *Maybe* Professor Singh will be absent.

May be is a verb: She *may be* at a conference.

moral (say *MORE al*), **morale** (say *more AL*). *Moral* (as an adjective) means "righteous, ethical": To pay his debts was a *moral* obligation. *Moral* (as a noun) means "a lesson or truth taught in a story": The *moral* of the story is that greed is wrong.

Morale (noun) means "spirit": The team's *morale* sagged after its 42–0 loss.

notable, notorious. See *famous*.

number. See *amount*.

one another. See *each other*.

oral. See *verbal*.

party, person. See *individual*.

passed, past. *Passed* (verb) is from *pass*: I *passed* the test. Our tour bus *passed* the museum without stopping.

Past (noun) means "former time": Forget the *past*. *Past* (preposition) means "by, beyond": Walk *past* it.

percent, percentage. Use *percent* with a specific figure: 45 *percent*. Otherwise, use *percentage*: a small *percentage* of voters.

> *Note:* The percentage is singular: *The percentage* of defaults *is* small. *A percentage* is either singular or plural, depending on what follows: *A percentage* of the fruit *is* spoiled. *A percentage* of the students *are* here.

personal (say *PER son al*), **personnel** (say *per son ELL*). *Personal* means "private": This is a *personal* matter, not a public one.

Personnel are formal members of a group, such as employees of a company: Notify all *personnel*.

persuade. See *convince*.

practical, practicable. *Practical* means "useful, sensible, not theoretical"; *practicable* means "feasible, capable of being put into practice": *Practical* people with *practical* experience can produce a *practicable* plan.

precede, proceed. To *precede* is to come before: X *precedes* Y.

Proceed means "to go forward": The parade *proceeded* along Main Street.

presence, presents. *Presence* means "being present; attendance": Their *presence* at the rally was noted.

Presents are gifts, such as birthday *presents*.

principle, principal. A *principle* is a rule or a truth (remember: *principLE* = *ruLE*): The Ten Commandments are moral *principles*. Some mathematical *principles* are difficult to grasp.

Elsewhere, use *principal*, meaning "chief, chief part, chief person": All *principal* roads are closed. At 3 percent, your *principal* [the main money you originally invested] will earn $30 interest. The *principal* addressed the students at graduation.

quiet, quite. *Quiet* means "not noisy": This motor is *quiet*.

Quite means "very, completely": I'm not *quite* ready.

raise, rise. *Raise, raised, raised* ("to lift; to make come up") is a transitive verb (needs an object): They *raise* tomatoes. The teacher *raised* the *window*. *Raise* our *salaries*!

Rise, rose, risen ("to ascend") is an intransitive verb (never has an object): The sun is *rising*. Salaries *rose*.

As a noun, generally use *rise*: Economists feared a *rise* in prices. (But, by custom, say a *raise* in salary.)

respectfully, respectively. *Respectfully* means "in a manner showing respect": Behave *respectfully* at worship. *Respectfully* yours.

Respectively means "each in the order given." Use it, when there is no better way, to clarify order: Brooks, McGee, and Black won in 2010, 2011, and 2012, *respectively*. But better: Brooks won the award in 2010, McGee in 2011, and Black in 2012.

right, rite, write. A *rite* is a ceremony: our initiation *rite*, a *rite* of passage into adulthood.

To *write* is to compose in words or music: *Write* us from India. Brahms didn't *write* a fifth symphony.

Elsewhere, use *right*: the *right* (correct) way, a *right* (not wrong) answer, a *right* (not left) turn, the *right* to vote.

sight, site. See *cite*.

sit, set. *Sit, sat, sat* is an intransitive verb (takes no object) meaning "to be seated": They *sat* on the floor.

Set, set, set is most commonly a transitive verb (needs an object) meaning "to put or place": She *set* her *book* on the desk. (*Set* is intransitive in certain uses: The sun *set* at 6:02. The hen is *setting* on her eggs.)

See a good dictionary for the many meanings of *set*.

stationary, stationery. *Stationary* means "not moving; not movable": The traffic jam kept our car *stationary* for an hour.

Stationery is writing paper.

take. See *bring*.

teach. See *learn*.

than, then. *Than* (conjunction) is used in comparing: She was more fit *than* he [was]. See 122C, page 17.

Then is an adverb meaning "at (or after) that time" or "in that case; therefore": They *then* went home. The vote may be tied; *then* the chairperson must decide.

that. See *who*.

their, there, they're. *Their* is a possessive pronoun: The litigants arrived with *their* lawyers. *Their* faces were tense.

There is an adverb of place: Sit *there*. It is also an expletive (an introductory word): *There* is no hope.

They're is a contraction of *they are*: *They're* having a party.

See 122A, page 17, and 122F, page 18.

threw, through. *Threw* is the past of *throw*. I *threw* the ball. For *through*, see next entry.

through (say *THROO*), **thorough** (say *THURR oh*). *Through* means "from end to end or side to side of": *through* the tunnel. It can also mean "finished." He was *through* with work.

Thorough means "complete, exact": a *thorough* search.

to, too, two. *To* is a preposition: They drove *to* Miami. *To* also introduces an infinitive: They wanted *to* find work.

Too is an adverb meaning "also" or "excessively": They met her *too*. He was *too* old to care. Do not use *too* for *very*: She didn't seem *very* happy (not *too happy*).

Two is a number: Take *two* of these pills.

toward, towards. Americans prefer *toward*; the British, *towards*.

uninterested. See *disinterested*.

verbal, oral. Strictly, *verbal* means "expressed in words, either written or spoken": Many computer programs use pictorial instead of *verbal* commands. (For the grammatical term *verbal*, see 117, page 12.)

Oral means "spoken": Give *oral*, not written, responses.

weak, week. *Weak* means "not strong": *weak* from the flu.

A *week* is seven days.

weather, whether. *Weather* refers to rain, sunshine, and so forth.

Whether introduces alternatives: *whether* they win or lose. See also *if, whether*.

well. See 119C, page 14.

whether. See *if, whether; weather*.

which. See *who*.

while, though, whereas. The basic meaning of *while* is "during the time that." Avoid using it to mean *and, but, though,* or *whereas,* especially if two times are involved: This test proved negative, *whereas* (or *though* or *but,* but not *while*) last month's was positive.

who, which, that. Use *who* to refer to persons; use *which* only for things; use *that* for things or persons. The player *who* [or *that,* but not *which*] scores lowest wins. See 121B, page 16.

who, whom. See 122D, E, pages 17–18.

whose, who's. *Whose* is the possessive of *who*: *Whose* hat is this?

Who's is the contraction of *who is*: *Who's* that? See 122F, page 18.

woman, women. *Woman* (say *WUHM an*) is singular, like *man*: That *woman* is here.

Women (say *WIMM en*) is plural, like *men*: Those *women* are here.

write. See *right, rite, write*.

your, you're. *Your* is the possessive of *you*: Wear *your* hat.

You're is a contraction of *you are*: *You're* late. See 122F, page 18.

For resources to help you master this section's topics, log in to www.mywritinglab.com and select Easily Confused Words from the list of subtopics.

PART 5 (Sections 501–510) Paragraphs and Papers

Most sentences that you write will become parts of larger units of writing—paragraphs—and most paragraphs will become parts of still larger units—essays, letters, emailings, Internet postings, papers, articles, and so forth. This final part of *English Simplified*, after presenting some pointers on manuscript form, explains the basics of writing paragraphs, emails, essays, and research papers, and surveys research paper documentation.

501. Manuscript Form

501A. Typeface. In keyboarding, choose a plain font, such as Times New Roman or Courier, and a type size of 10 or 12 points (see samples in 510, page 75). Do not use boldface.

501B. Spacing. Use double spacing and be sure margins are one inch all around (see 510, page 75). Indent each new paragraph five spaces or one tab stroke. Do not indent the first line of a page unless it begins a paragraph. Do not leave extra space between paragraphs or leave one line of a paragraph alone at the top or bottom of a page.

Quotations. Separate from the text any prose quotations longer than four lines or verse quotations longer than three lines; use no quotation marks; indent (from left margin) ten spaces or two tab strokes; maintain double spacing.

Keep shorter quotations in the body of your text; enclose them in quotation marks; see 215I, page 38, and 508A, page 69.

501C. Titles and Page Numbers. For placing of titles, see 510A, page 75. For punctuation and capitalization of titles, see 205, page 35; 219A, page 39; and 301F, page 43.

Number all pages (1, 2 . . .) in the upper right corner, with no periods or parentheses. If using MLA style, precede each page number with your last name; if using APA, instead of your last name use a short form of your title. See 510, page 75, for examples.

501D. Corrections. Before handing in a paper, proofread it carefully (see 506B, page 65). If you have many errors, redo the page. If you have only a few minor errors, make changes neatly, as follows:

Deletions. Draw a horizontal line through words to be deleted. Do not use parentheses. See 224A, page 41.

Insertions. Above the line write the word(s) to be inserted, and just below the line use a caret (∧) to show the point of insertion.

Paragraphing. Use the ¶ sign to show the point at which you wish to begin a paragraph. Write *No* ¶ if you wish to remove a paragraph indention.

502–503. Paragraphs

Generally, a paragraph contains several sentences clearly related in meaning, developing a single topic. Paragraphs are also visual entities that reduce a page-long mass of print to smaller units that are more inviting to read.

Paragraphs vary greatly in function, structure, length, and style. A paragraph of **dialogue,** for example, may contain only a few words (each new speaker gets a new paragraph—see 215H, page 38). A **transitional** paragraph between main parts of a long paper may have only one or two sentences. The guidelines in sections 502 and 503 apply mainly to **body** paragraphs (those developing your main idea) of expository (explanatory), descriptive, and persuasive papers. **Introductory** and **concluding** paragraphs are shown in section 506, pages 66–67.

502. Paragraph Length.

ESL The length of a paragraph depends on the topic and its needed development. The typical paragraph may run four to eight sentences, though sometimes one or two important sentences deserve a paragraph of their own. If your paragraph gets too long, break it into shorter paragraphs at a logical dividing point, such as between major reasons or examples.

503. Paragraph Content

503A. The Topic Sentence. Develop your paragraph around a *single* main topic or idea, usually stated in one sentence called the **topic sentence.** Read paragraphs 1–6 on pages 60–62 to see how each topic sentence (boxed) controls the content of its paragraph. The other sentences ordinarily give evidence to support what the topic sentence asserts. Most often, you will place your topic sentence first—or just after an introductory or transitional sentence.

> ***Paragraph 1*** (topic sentence first)—about biological body cells:
>
> The wonder of cells is not that things occasionally go wrong, but that they manage everything so smoothly for decades at a stretch. They do so by constantly sending and monitoring streams of messages—a cacophony of messages—from all around the body: instructions, queries, corrections, requests for assistance, updates, notices to divide or expire. Most of these signals arrive by means of couriers called hormones, chemical entities such as insulin, adrenaline, estrogen, and testosterone that convey information from remote outposts like the thyroid and endocrine glands. Still other messages arrive by telegraph from the brain or from regional centers in a process called paracrine signaling. Finally, cells communicate directly with their neighbors to make sure their actions are coordinated.
>
> —Bill Bryson

You may sometimes place the topic sentence last, as a climax, with your supporting sentences leading up to it.

> ***Paragraph 2*** (topic sentence last)—from a student essay:
>
> Instead of going to college after high school, I traveled around the world with a band for about five years—New York, London, Paris, even Tokyo. I wanted

to experience what I thought was the glamorous life of a musician. During the first year I ventured out every night and met hundreds of new people. However, as the years of traveling wore on, I began to miss my friends and family. Even the thought of my hometown, which I had spent so much of my youth trying to flee, made me feel nostalgic. I began to envision Thanksgiving dinners with my parents at our old house, fishing in Alder Creek, meeting my school buddies at the Empire Diner downtown. Soon I realized that even though our band was doing well playing shows, we were not really going anywhere. I decided that our next show, in Amsterdam, would be my last and booked a flight back to Oregon. Although I look back on those days with no regrets, I am ultimately satisfied with my decision to settle down, go back to school, and study music education, a path that I hope will allow me to share the joy of music with others.

In addition to an opening topic sentence, you may provide a conclusion, or **clincher sentence,** that sums up your thinking on the topic, as in the following paragraph.

> ***Paragraph 3*** (topic and clincher sentences)—from a student essay:
>
> The beautiful and lush Hiroshima Peace Park in Japan is meant to memorialize the 1945 atomic bombing by promoting peace and hope. This optimistic approach to coping with tragedy epitomizes the act of remembrance. Merely mourning tragic past events with a traditional somber statue is not an appropriate use of a memorial site. Rather, places that promote positive change and healing are the best way to memorialize a person or event. The Peace Park occupies the open field where the nuclear blast flattened scores of buildings and ended so many lives; now the area is filled with gorgeous plant life and rows of flowering trees. The idea that life thrives where tens of thousands of deaths occurred symbolizes the endurance of Japanese people, their culture, and their yearning for peace, more so than would any monument of stone.

Occasionally you may need more than one full sentence—or less than a full one—to state your topic. Experienced writers sometimes just imply a topic sentence.

503B. Adequate Development. All other sentences in your paragraph should support the general idea you state in your topic sentence. Many inexperienced writers fail to develop their paragraphs fully enough; they may merely paraphrase the main idea several times or add vague generalizations instead of convincing, detailed evidence. Compare the development in paragraphs 4A and 4B below, both about Alaska. Which writer better convinces you of what the topic sentence asserts?

> ***Paragraph 4A***
>
> Our family has always lived on Douglas Island. We had to walk a couple of miles to catch the school bus. We would row across the channel to run errands or to attend the Russian Orthodox Church in Juneau. My family was very involved in church activities. My siblings and I went to church school, where I tried to learn to read prayers in Russian. I have always liked learning new things.

> ***Paragraph 4B***
>
> Our family has lived for five (now starting six) generations on a small piece of land on Douglas Island, across the Gastineau Channel from Juneau. There was no road when I was a child, so we had to walk along the beach for about half an hour to meet the school bus. Taxis would also drop us off at that point. Before the Juneau–Douglas bridge was finished in the mid-1930s, the family would row across the channel to shop, go to movies, or go to church. The family believed in a higher power, and my uncle set aside time for prayer wherever we were. On Sunday, we all rowed across for services at St. Nicolas Orthodox Church. Whenever we were in Hoonah, we were also active in church activities, especially meetings and choir practice. Often these were held in the clan houses. When we went to church school, I tried to learn to read Russian prayers. As I look back on things, I guess I had the desire to go to school all along.
>
> —Nora Marks Dauenhauer

Put enough specific evidence in your paragraph to support your main idea strongly, convincing even skeptical readers of what your topic sentence asserts.

Ways of development. For each paragraph, choose the most appropriate way(s) to present your support, such as with

- **Facts** or **examples** (see all the sample paragraphs)
- One or more **reasons** (paragraphs 2, 5—pages 60, 62)
- Elements of a **description** (paragraph 4B), **definition** (5), or **explanation** (1, 3, 5, 6)
- A sequence of **time** (paragraph 2), **process** (1), or **cause–effect** (5)
- Points of **comparison** or **contrast** (paragraphs 3, 6). A special kind of comparison is an **analogy** (clarifying a concept by comparing it to something familiar); paragraph 1, for example, likens cell communication to human communication with the words *requests for assistance . . . couriers . . . remote outposts . . . telegraph . . . neighbors.*

503C. Coherence. Your paragraphs *cohere* (hold together well) when you clearly signal or imply how your ideas relate to one another—when your thought flows smoothly from the first sentence through the last (and from one paragraph to the next). You can achieve coherence by using (1) a controlling structure, (2) transitions, and (3) repeated key words or phrases.

A controlling structure. Think of a structure—a skeleton—around which to build a paragraph. Such a structure can be as simple as labeling your reasons *first, second,* and *third* (try climactic order—build from less important reasons to the most important).

Paragraph 2, for example, is structured around leaving and returning; paragraph 4B, around the two places in the family's home life; paragraph 6, around contrasts in terminology.

Transitional expressions make both your meaning and your structure clearer: | ESL

Purpose	Examples
Show time relationships	before, after[ward], previously, formerly, meanwhile, at last, simultaneously, until then
Indicate stages of thought	first [*not* firstly], second, then, next, finally
Introduce particulars	for example, for instance, in particular
Show cause or effect	consequently, as a result, because of these
Signal further evidence	in addition, moreover, furthermore, also
Mark a contrast or change of direction	however, yet, but, still, on the other hand, nevertheless
Show other relationships	above all, that is, likewise, similarly, more important
Signal a conclusion	therefore, thus, then, on the whole, in sum (*avoid the trite* in conclusion)

You may use all or part of a sentence for transition, either at the beginning of your paragraph or within it:

> But the new science could not rely on these pioneers alone. . . .
>
> Despite such difficulties . . .
>
> Nor is depression the only effect. . . .
>
> In appearance . . . In actuality . . .

Repetition of key words or phrases gives your reader signposts to follow your train of thought. A repetition may consist of the word itself, a synonym, or a pronoun referring to the word, such as *these, that, which,* or *such.* Repeating a familiar term from the preceding sentence near the beginning of your new sentence works especially well. Check these repeated terms in paragraphs 1–6:

- *In paragraph 1* (page 60): *messages* (similar words: *signals, signaling, communicate*)
- *In paragraph 2* (page 60): words of going (*traveled, world, ventured, flee*) and returning (*hometown, nostalgic, settle down*)
- *In paragraph 3* (page 61): *peace (healing), remembering (memorialize), tragedy, statue, lush (gorgeous)*
- *In paragraph 5* (below): *disorder, image, ritual (behavior)*
- *In paragraph 6* (below): *work (jobs), euphemism (promiscuously used language), society (they, others)*

See how paragraphs 5 and 6 each begin with a transition linking the paragraph to the preceding paragraph in its book (*Yet another type* . . . in paragraph 5, . . . *in such surreal circumstances* . . . in paragraph 6), and how each

paragraph is held together by transitions (italicized) and repeated words and expressions (boldfaced).*

Paragraph 5

Yet another type of anxiety **disorder** is the **obsessive-compulsive disorder.** With **this,** disturbing ideas or **images** flood the person's mind—**this** is the **obsessive** part of the **disorder.** The sufferer *then* creates routine, repetitive **rituals** to rid the mind of **these images.** One of the most famous characters in theatrical literature depicting an **obsessive-compulsive disorder** is Lady Macbeth in Shakespeare's *Macbeth.* Lady Macbeth saw the **image** of blood on her hands after she committed a murder. She washed her hands again and again to rid herself of the feeling of guilt associated with **this** mental **image.** Her hand-washing, of course, had no effect whatsoever—it was a meaningless and **repetitious behavior** because it did not absolve her of her guilt. **Such** a routine and repeated **ritual** is the **compulsive** part of an **obsessive-compulsive disorder.**

—Don Colbert

Paragraph 6

Is it any wonder that in such surreal circumstances, **status** rather than the **work** itself becomes important? *Thus* the prevalence of **euphemisms** in **work** as well as in war. The **janitor** is a **building engineer;** the **garbage man,** a **sanitary engineer;** the **man at the rendering plant,** a **factory mechanic;** the **gravedigger,** a **caretaker. They** are not **themselves** ashamed of **their work,** *but* **society, they** feel, looks upon **them** as a lesser species. *So* **they** call upon **promiscuously used language** to match the "respectability" of **others,** whose **jobs** may have less **social worth** than **their** own.

—Studs Terkel

503D. Unity and Emphasis. Unity means that every sentence must fit precisely within your stated topic. Suppose paragraph 1 (page 60) had ended like this:

> The body's 206 bones also help keep each of us functioning throughout life. Both strong bones and good cell communication are needed for a healthy body.

Such sentences would ruin the paragraph's unity because they introduce a new topic—bones—not covered by the topic sentence.

Emphasis means that your main points get the most space—standing out clearly, not lost in a clutter of unexplained detail.

Using *a controlling structure, transitional expressions,* and *key repetitions* not only aids coherence but also helps preserve unity and emphasis.

For resources to help you master this section's topics, log in to www.mywritinglab.com and select Recognizing the Paragraph and Developing and Organizing a Paragraph from the list of subtopics.

---

*Italics and boldface added by the authors of *English Simplified.*

504. Netiquette Guidelines

504. Writing Effectively Online. In an email, Facebook entry, blog, or other online posting, follow these **rules:**

- Consider your **subject** and **audience.**
- Always include a **subject line.**
- Use **appropriate language.** (See 402 A, B, page 52.)
- Offer a polite **greeting and closing.** Use *Hi, . . .* only for friends; for business emails, most authorities favor using the traditional *Dear . . .*; for other email, consider *Good morning, . . .* or *Hello, ...*
- Be **brief** and **clear** about your point.
- Adjust the **formality** of your tone as necessary.
- **Edit** and **proofread** your text as necessary.
- Never resort to **cyberbullying** or **flaming** (profanity, name calling, and the like). Avoid sending **confidential** messages. Say nothing that would cause a problem if others besides your recipient were to see it. (Read the sample essay in 506C, page 66.)
- Use **emoticons** (a group of keyboard characters that represent facial expressions, such as :-) for a smile) for informal messages only.
- **Proofread** carefully before sending.
- Always **respond promptly.**

> *Note:* When using Facebook or other social networking sites such as Twitter or Flickr, use privacy settings to monitor what can be viewed by other users (profile, photos, videos, postings). Do not provide highly personal information about yourself or others (addresses, phone numbers, and the like).

ESL

505–506. Essays

Just as you build related sentences into paragraphs, you build related paragraphs into longer pieces of writing. One kind—perhaps two to four pages long in college—is an **essay.** Essays allow you to ponder and evaluate your own life experiences, observations, thinking, reading, media experiences, and imagination to convey your ideas on just about any kind of topic.

505. Before Starting to Write

505A. Choosing and Limiting Your Topic. If you are allowed to choose your own topic or if you are assigned a broad subject, such as campus life, you will have to narrow, or limit, your topic to one that (1) lies within your interests, knowledge, and available resources, (2) should interest your readers, and (3) can be treated adequately within the given length and deadline.

Too broad:	Life on campus
	Race relations in college
	The rise of social media sites
Limited:	City slicker at a rural campus
	Sharing an interracial dorm room
	Having a disagreement with a friend over the Internet

One long-range approach to choosing a topic is to keep a **journal** (a daily record) of your experiences and observations. September journal entries can lead to effective December essays.

505B. Planning Your Essay. Start early and maintain a disciplined schedule so that you will not have to submit a rush job. Along the way, if an idea is not working out or if a much better one hits you, revise your topic, your central idea (thesis), or your outline.

Preliminary considerations

Your audience. To whom are you writing? Your instructor, of course, but probably also your classmates—or perhaps readers of the campus newspaper. Consider your audience's probable knowledge of your subject and attitudes toward it; fit your content and *voice*—word choice, sentence structure, tone—to your audience.

Your purpose. Do you want to *explain* the why or how of your topic (exposition)? To *persuade* your audience to think or act differently? To *describe* or *tell* (narrate) something important?

Prewriting. How do you fashion a headful of jumbled thoughts and facts into a coherent essay? Try one or more of these ways, or create your own:

Brainstorming. Just write, nonstop, a *list* of whatever enters your mind on your subject. Do not pause to evaluate or rethink anything, no matter how far-out it seems. Then choose your most promising ideas and begin working with them. You may brainstorm either with others or by yourself.

Freewriting. Try *freewriting* if you have difficulty starting. Just start writing, nonstop, *sentences* on anything even loosely related to your subject. Repeat if you have to. Eventually, your mind should unlock thoughts on your subject.

Mapping (clustering). Write your subject or tentative topic in the center of a page. Then, around it, jot down ideas and facts as they come to you; circle each one—bigger or heavier circles for broader ideas. Draw lines between the central subject and the big circles, then between each big circle and the smaller circles that relate to it. Cross out dead-end circles that you find connect nowhere.

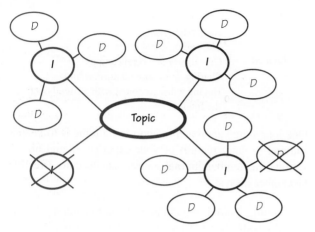

I = broad idea *D* = supporting detail or evidence
Crossed-out circles = items found to be irrelevant

Questioning. Like a newspaper reporter, ask yourself *who, what, when, where, why,* and *how* about your topic.

505C. Forming a Thesis. Your essay must not be a mere pile of facts about a topic. Pondering your jotted-down facts and ideas should lead you toward one controlling idea, or point, that you want to convey: your **thesis** (what your essay would say if boiled down to one sentence). Write a **thesis sentence** stating this point. Be sure the sentence asserts something about your topic (says what you will *show* about your topic).

A thesis is *not* merely a restatement of the topic. Nor is it a stale statement of something rather obvious, such as *We must keep our nation secure against terrorists.* A thesis presents a reasonably original point that can arouse readers' interest, stimulate their thought, and perhaps generate lively discussion.

Paths to a good thesis. One path is to ask yourself a key question, such as "What did I learn from sharing a dorm room with a person of another race?" The answer can become your thesis: "Sharing a biracial dorm room breaks down racial preconceptions, brings understanding, and can lead to friendship." (These three effects of sharing can become the divisions of the body of your essay; see 506A, page 65.)

Another way to form a thesis is to complete this sentence: *In this essay I will show that. . . .* The words following *show that* will form a thesis sentence (in your actual essay, drop the words *In this essay I will show that*): ~~In this essay I will show that~~ all of us, both as individuals and members of organizations, must buttress recognized legal limits with our own ethical limits on information we make publicly available online.

Qualities of a good thesis sentence. A good thesis sentence (1) focuses on *one worthwhile, interest-arousing* assertion, (2) promises a *fresh insight* into or *deeper*

understanding of the topic, and (3) can be *convincingly supported* by your facts and logic.

Compare these thesis sentences:

Unworkable	Workable
This campus is becoming increasingly multiracial. [just a fact or observation] Campus racial harmony is desirable. [too broad, stale, unarguable]	Increasingly strong bonds between whites and Asians on our campus are only further alienating other minorities. [limited, original, insightful]
Nearly everyone on this campus is a racist. [too broad, unsupportable]	To create a nonthreatening learning environment at our college, the administration must take the lead in eliminating racial bias. [limited, supportable]

505D. Choosing an Approach. Your purpose and thesis will determine the way in which you organize your ideas. Here are the most common approaches:

- **Narrations** generally follow time order (e.g., my victory over cancer). Explanations of a **process** (laying tracks in recording music) also use time order. Be sure to clarify any technical terms.
- **Descriptions** use spatial order (a strip mine). Be sure to move consistently: left → right; far → near; outside → center; or in some similar logical progression.
- **Explanations** (why some prefer music on old vinyl LPs) are open to many kinds of order, such as simple → complex; familiar → unfamiliar; or analogy (see 503B, page 61, for definition).
- **Definitions** (the true meaning of *liberal*)
- **Classifications** or **divisions** (types of people one meets at a bar)
- **Comparisons** or **contrasts** (Republican and Democratic solutions to recession) can proceed by either (1) presenting all of one side of the issue, then all of the other (first the Republicans' ideas, then the Democrats') or (2) —often better— presenting each side's ideas alternately, point by point (unemployment, inflation, government's role . . .).
- **Cause–effect** papers can move from effect (acid rain) to cause(s) or from cause (more couples over thirty-five having children) to effect(s).
- **Persuasive** (argumentative) papers (vote for the Green Party this fall) try to change readers' thinking on an issue. Move from your least convincing point to your most convincing.
- **Problem–solution** papers (see sample essay, page 66).

505E. Outlining. An outline helps you determine the sequence and relative importance of your ideas. After deciding on your approach, make some kind of tentative outline of your essay (stay flexible—change it as needed). At the beginning of any outline, write your thesis sentence.

A scratch outline. Just jot down your main points in order. Leave ample space between each; in the space below each main point, list supporting items (indented). A variation of this outline is the **topic sentence outline:** write the topic sentence you intend for each paragraph. (The scratch outline is good also for in-class, timed essays and examination essay questions.)

A tree outline lets you see clearly where each of your points or supporting details fits best and how sound your overall structure is:

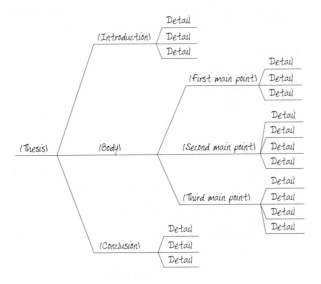

A formal outline clarifies the sequence and relative importance of ideas, using numbers, letters, and indenting. Your instructor may require one. (You might want to build it from a preliminary scratch or tree outline):

Thesis: All of us, both as individuals and members of organizations, must buttress recognized legal limits with our own ethical limits on information we make publicly available online.

I. The problem: Unprecedented impact of social networks
  A. Worldwide political effects
  B. Interpersonal effects
II. Negative personal effect of one social message
  A. Causes
    1. Illusion of distance and confidentiality
    2. Consequent irresponsible behavior
  B. Events
    1. Friend's message about me
    2. Forwarding of message to me
  C. Result: sense of betrayal, anger
. . . [Outline continues]

Maintain parallel structure in a formal outline. See 128F, page 25.

506. Writing and Revising the Essay

506A. Writing the First Draft. Essays have three parts: introduction, body, and conclusion. (See example, 506C, page 66.)

The introduction (usually one paragraph) arouses reader interest, presents the topic and often the thesis, and may suggest the essay's organization. You may arouse interest with a *surprising fact* (half of America's children live in nontraditional families), a *question* (what can account for our endless fascination with UFOs?), an *anecdote* (one day last week I saw . . .), or a *common assumption that you will challenge* (we take for granted that America's roads are the world's best).

The body develops the thesis in several paragraphs (usually three or more). What you learned about writing good paragraphs (adequate development, coherence, unity, and emphasis—section 503) applies equally here. Your thesis sentence may suggest the divisions of your paper's body (similarity of students' [1] *goals,* [2] *ages,* and [3] *interests* encourages racial harmony).

The conclusion should (re)emphasize your thesis. It may briefly restate your main points and may make a prediction or suggest action. A good conclusion ends with a strong sentence that both signals "the end" and keeps readers thinking about what you have shown.

506B. Revising, Editing, and Proofreading. A good essay is usually the product of several drafts and revisions. Use the checklist on page 66 to improve your drafts and polish the final paper. In writing your early drafts, do not stop to edit for grammar, mechanics, or style; keep your thoughts flowing. When possible, have one or more classmates read your drafts for feedback and proofread your final paper.

Editing-proofreading hints:

- One read-through is not enough. Proofread slowly, with concentration, several times.
- Remember that most computer spelling checkers do not catch homonyms (*there* for *their*) or wrong words correctly spelled (*clam* for *calm*), and that grammar-style checkers are often imprecise.
- If possible, read your paper into a recording device and listen to the playback as you proofread.
- Do one proofing backward, from last sentence to first, to catch sentence-structure errors.
- Do another proofing backward, word by word, to catch spelling errors and repeated or omitted words.

506C. Sample Student Essay. The following sample is a **problem-solution** paper. The **introduction** briefly states the issue and defines the paper's scope. The writer does not give the paper's thesis here; he wants the reader to follow his line of reasoning leading up to the thesis, which

---

CHECKLIST

1. **Revising drafts.** Focus on content:
   - *Introduction:* interest-arousing? topic made clear? leading smoothly into body?
   - *Thesis:* clear, appropriate, limited, provable?
   - *Supporting evidence:* sufficient? more specifics needed? free of unsupported generalizations? unbiased? in logical order?
   - *Unity:* everything on topic—no drifting off? free of extraneous or redundant statements?
   - *Coherence:* ideas in logical order? each point leading clearly to the next?
   - *Emphasis:* main points clearly led up to and given most space?
   - *Conclusion:* following logically from thesis and supporting evidence in body? not too broad? ending strong?

2. **Editing.** Focus on sentences and wording:
   - *Paragraph structure:* topic sentences clear? other sentences clearly related to them?
   - *Sentences:* varied in length, type, wording? strong, effective?
   - *Word choice, tone, degree of formality:* appropriate to topic and audience? word meanings clear for readers? concise, specific? nondiscriminatory?
   - *Flow of thought:* made clear by transitional expressions, repetition of key words?

3. **Proofreading.** Focus on details of correctness:
   - *Keyboarding:* text free of unintentionally repeated or omitted words, etc.?
   - *Manuscript form:* correct margins, spacing, indentations, etc. (see section 501)?
   - *Grammar:* correct pronoun reference, modifier placement, sentence structure, agreement, etc.? clarity throughout?
   - *Punctuation:* correct, adequate, conveying meaning clearly?
   - *Mechanics and spelling:* capitalization, etc. correct and consistent?
   - *Usage:* free of confused words?

---

he withholds until the **conclusion**. (Topic sentence of each paragraph is in italics.)

In the **body**, paragraphs 2–4 relate the central incident, showing how its consequences exemplify the overall problem. Paragraph 5 presents the positive side of the issue.

The **conclusion**, paragraph 6, sums up the effect of the problem on the writer, restates the problem, and leads the reader into the **thesis** (in bold), giving the writer's solution to the problem—what must be done. The essay ends with a pithy, easily remembered sentence that neatly ties up everything.*

Caught in the Social Network Dilemma

In the few years of their existence, Facebook, Twitter, and similar social networking Internet sites have had a seismic effect on both the social and political worlds. On a global scale, the revolutionary protests beginning in 2011 in Egypt and elsewhere in the Arab world are known to have been organized to a great extent via Facebook, as young men and women, having discovered on the Internet how democracy can work, have taken action to achieve it for themselves. On an interpersonal scale as well, social networking has profoundly affected individual and group relationships—not always for the better, as I recently found out.

Facebook, Twitter, and the like, eliminating face-to-face contact and lacking tangible boundaries or apparent consequences, create the illusion of distance and thus of confidentiality between users; this can translate into an excuse for behaving badly. Until earlier this year I had paid little attention to stories about damaging and slanderous personal information being spread online. Then I suddenly found myself enmeshed in a serious conflict with a friend because of the Web. One night the friend, Brandon, stayed over at my house. While I was asleep he instant-messaged my girlfriend, Brooke. I was unaware of this until another friend, Andy, shared the information, which was about me and quite derogatory, by forwarding it to me on Facebook. Brandon had pasted his message to Brooke into his message to Andy, making what he thought was confidential available to others on this friend-to-friend network. I felt betrayed and angry.

Brandon doubtless did not fully comprehend the risk he took when he instant-messaged Brooke and Andy. I discovered later that not only had he asked Brooke to break up with me immediately, so that he and she could be together, but he had also made disparaging comments about my personality and appearance. Relayed to me through Andy, all this was proof that he was trying to break up my relationship with Brooke. To their credit, Brooke and Andy both felt obligated to let me know the truth about my "best friend." Brandon's use of a social network enabled them to show me the actual text as evidence of his deceit.

Ironically, the physical evidence that the Internet makes available dismantles the Web's illusion of confidentiality. Once a person clicks *Send, Post,* or *Enter,* that action cannot be undone; the posted information becomes permanently, indelibly available to all sharers of a site. When I finally confronted Brandon, he could not deny what he had said; I had the printout in my hand. Surprisingly, he did not apologize or even admit that his actions were wrong. On the contrary, he felt that his own sense of privacy had been violated, because he had assumed that his message to Andy would go no further. The outcome of our confrontation was the ending of our friendship—or what I had thought was a friendship.

---

*Italics and boldface added by the authors of *English Simplified*.

My experience, though trivial compared with the hatred, violence, and public disgrace that some Facebook and Twitter entries have caused, made me ponder to what extent such networks should be subject to controls. Should they be censored or even shut down because of their potential for harm? By no means, I realized. *These tools can also bring people and communities together through the sharing of information and ideas, and can dispel false beliefs.* As we have seen in North Africa and the Middle East, Facebook allows users to cross geographical and political boundaries effortlessly, establishing and nourishing friendships and exchanging news and pictures throughout the world, penetrating oppressive regimes to spread ideas of democracy, equality, and, hopefully, peace.

Though Brandon's duplicity upset and angered me (even if it had the silver lining of my learning the truth), it has taught me the potential damage of sharing private information, especially negative comments, over the social networks. Both network and civil authorities are, rightly, attempting to solve this problem through stricter privacy regulations and laws such as those against cyberbullying. Perhaps personal lawsuits can help end Internet slander. In the long run, however, we must all consider the consequences of what we ourselves say online, exercising both caution and restraint. **You, I, everyone, both as individuals and in our organizations, must buttress recognized legal limits with our own ethical limits on information we make available online.** On the social networks, say nothing about a person that you would not say to that person face to face (and believe nothing about a person just because someone has said it online). The social media are neither good nor bad; their free, effective future depends in the long run on each user's personal integrity— yours and mine.

For resources to help you master this section's topics, log in to www.mywritinglab.com and select Recognizing the Essay and Essay Organization from the list of subtopics.

507–510. Research Papers

507. Planning and Researching. Unlike most class essays, research papers are based largely on data gathered from libraries, computer-based sources, and sometimes interviews or other field research. The great amount of work involved demands that you start early, set up a workable schedule, and adhere to it strictly. Rarely are *A* papers written at 4 a.m. on deadline day.

507A. Choosing and Limiting a Topic. What was said for essays (section 505A, page 63) applies even more here: narrow your focus. *Dangers to our national parks* is a book-length topic, but *the snowmobile controversy in our*

northern national parks fits research-paper length. You can limit a topic by

- ***Taking part of the whole:*** Choose one of Hemingway's short stories rather than a whole range of them.
- ***Restricting time, place, or both:*** not *modern American relations with the Middle East* but *why the U.S. left Iraq's Saddam regime in power after the 1991 war.*

A topic must be researchable, not based primarily on personal experience or speculation; it must lend itself to objective, even-handed treatment leading to a conclusion based solidly on your evidence; it must be completable with resources available to you. You will need perhaps ten or more sources, never just one or two.

507B. Forming a Thesis. Follow the guidelines for essays, section 505C, page 64. In particular, try forming a question that your research can answer. Remember that your initial thesis is tentative and will probably be revised as your research progresses.

507C. Locating Sources

Print sources include general and reference books, periodicals (magazines, newspapers, journals), and government documents. Locate books through your library's computerized catalog. If you find few or no books on your exact topic (e.g., *the sense of place of the Tlingit tribe*), look under broader or related topics (e.g., *Native American tribes of the Pacific Northwest*). You may find a book with some information on your topic; check its index, and scan its bibliography for further sources.

General reference works. Encyclopedias, almanacs, and other reference works, such as the *Dictionary of American Biography,* are good places to begin research on many topics.

Indexes. Most usable periodical articles are listed in periodical indexes, such as the *New York Times Index* and the *Reader's Guide to Periodical Literature,* and subject indexes, such as the *Social Sciences Index, MLA Bibliography,* and *Education Index.* Such indexes are usually online or on CD-ROMs.

Electronic sources have become as important as printed ones, especially for recent information. Such sources include ***TV and radio programs, podcasts, films, video and audio tapes, videos posted on the Web, CDs, DVDs, and CD-ROMs*** (compact computer discs of encyclopedias, indexes, and much else).

Online sources of all kinds: indexes, abstracts or full texts of articles or books, newspapers from many nations; newsgroups; blogs; discussion groups; and countless other sites accessible through their Internet addresses (URLs) or through search engines such as Google, Yahoo!, or Bing (but see "Special cautions" in 507E).

Keyword searches. To look for sources (do a **keyword search**) with a search engine, type your topic in the Search or similar box on the computer screen. The *Library of Congress Subject Headings* can help you find the best keywords for your topic. Put + or *AND* (depending on the engine) before words you want included, and – or *NOT* before those you want excluded:

> *malaria + drug + treatment – quinine*
> *malaria AND drug AND treatment NOT quinine*

Use quotation marks around words you want searched as a group (*"Internet social networking"*—otherwise, you may get too broad a range of results). To broaden your search, use *OR,* especially for closely related terms (*"social networking sites" OR "social networking tools"*); to narrow a search, add more specific terms (+ *Facebook* + *Twitter*) or exclude some (– *YouTube*).

Field work. Some topics lend themselves to gathering original data through interviews, questionnaires, or objective direct observation (such as observing behavior of passers-by toward homeless people begging on the sidewalk). You may interview an authority in person, by phone, or electronically. In an interview or questionnaire, make your questions concise, specific, to the point, objective, and easily answerable in a usable form.

507D. The Working Bibliography. Use MLA, APA, or any other style your instructor directs. You may also consider consulting *NoodleBib* or *EasyBib,* databases that will guide you in generating citations for MLA, APA, and other styles. The items you eventually use will need to be arranged in a single alphabetical list.

507E. Evaluating Your Sources. Not all sources you find will be equally reliable. Reliability depends on

Type of publication. Avoid tabloid newspapers and most newsstand magazines as well as publications that seem to be pushing a type of product (such as some health-fitness magazines). Your college library is the best place to find reliable print sources. Scholarly journals and books from university presses are generally the most reliable, but also acceptable are favorably reviewed general books and reputable periodicals such as the *Atlantic Monthly, Scientific American, Time,* the *New York Times,* and the *Wall Street Journal.* But see "Objectivity" below.

Author's expertise. Choose an author such as a professor or well-known expert in the field in preference to a general journalist or freelancer; look for her credentials on the book jacket or accompanying the article. And see that she gives sources for her facts. Look for a bibliography and an index.

Recency. Be sure your sources are up to date, except when an older work is a classic or basic study in its field.

Objectivity. With few exceptions (such as rigidly scientific studies), each source will reflect its author's leanings on the subject. Find and present a fair balance of viewpoints on your topic. Distinguish between fact and opinion or assertion. (Fact: Americans buy millions of packs of chewing gum each year. Opinion/assertion: gum chewers make a poor impression on others). Be alert for one-sided arguments and unsupported claims. Be wary of data from sources advocating a cause or a product. ("Sixty-two percent of Americans do not chew enough gum." Who says so? How was this determined? What is "enough"?)

Special cautions for Internet sources. Though the Internet contains many highly reliable sources, it is a largely ungoverned system: anyone can say almost anything— perhaps slanted, defamatory, or wholly false. Web sites ending in *.edu* or *.gov* are generally reliable. Sites with *.org* (nonprofit groups) and *.com* (profit-seeking companies) range from quite reliable (the *New York Times*) to highly biased (a political party's site). For most topics, be wary of biased or false information on blogs; ask your instructor whether a particular blog is reliable. *Wikipedia* and the like (referred to as *wikis*) are open to anyone to contribute information; supposedly, other users will correct errors, but this cannot be ensured.

> *Note:* Many online sources periodically change their data; write down the date of the site's latest update and the date you accessed the site.

507F. Taking Notes. Note-taking and planning go hand in hand. With a clear plan you will do less unnecessary reading and note-taking; and as your knowledge of the topic grows, you can sharpen your plan. In taking notes you may (1) quote directly, (2) paraphrase (see below), or (3) summarize what the source says. Quote sparingly; your paper should be mostly your own words.

Take notes on a set of index cards or laptop entries separate from your bibliography list, because notes need to be arranged in topic order but bibliography items alphabetically. Record the page number (if any) of the information, and key each note to its corresponding bibliography item (e.g., write "McCulloch, *John Adams* 287" on the note).

A paraphrase is a restatement of source material in your own words. It is longer and more detailed than a summary. It must

- Acknowledge the source.
- Be entirely in your own words and sentence structure (if you just cannot restate a phrase, quote it).
- Use the same general order as the source.
- Not contain your own ideas or comments.

Unacceptable paraphrase of part of paragraph 6, page 62—fails to mention the source, stays too close to source's wording (italicized), and inserts student's comment ("This is a result . . ."):

> In the *surreal circumstances* of postmodern society, it is *no wonder that status rather than work itself is more important* in the professional world. This is the result of advanced technology and a rise in the number of college graduates. *Janitors* are *building engineers, garbage men* are *sanitary engineers*, and so on. These people are not necessarily *ashamed of their work, but society, they feel,* looks upon them as a lesser species. As a result they use certain terms *to match the respectability of others, whose jobs* have more *social worth than their own.*

Acceptable paraphrase:

> Terkel maintains that the blue-collar workforce has been subordinated by the rise of the professional classes. People with certain blue-collar jobs have been assigned lengthier titles, as "euphemisms" for their supposedly less valuable contribution to society. This is meant to give their jobs more value in relation to white-collar jobs, but the result is that the blue-collar workers are devalued and stripped of their "social worth."

See also 508B, page 70.

507G. Pulling Everything Together. When finished taking notes, look over your data and revise your outline, thesis, or both, as needed. Arrange your notes in an order matching your outline and start writing your first draft. All that has been said about good paragraphs (502–503, pages 60–62) and essays (505–506, pages 63–67) applies here as well.

508. Citing Sources Accurately.
Research papers, many reports, and articles for publication require **documentation** of all information obtained from books, periodicals, and other outside sources. Documentation consists of (1) **citations**—acknowledgments, at the point of use in your text, of the sources of material you have used and (2) a **references list**—an alphabetical list at the end of your paper of all the sources you used (also called a *works cited* list or a *bibliography*—see 509, pages 70–74). Papers in English, foreign language, and some other humanities require the Modern Language Association (MLA) style; those in the behavioral sciences and some other subjects use the American Psychological Association (APA) style.*

> *Note:* There is a modified form of both MLA and APA styles, called the Columbia Online Style (COS). It has been designed especially to accommodate electronic sources. If your instructor wants you to use this style, Google "Columbia Online Style."

508A. Citing Within the Paper. You must identify the sources of all facts and ideas, including opinions, that you obtain

from your research (exception: widely available facts, such as President Grant died in 1885 in upstate New York). You must tell enough about each source that your reader can locate the source and the information, and you must always make clear where the source material begins and ends in your text. (See 508B, "Avoiding Plagiarism," page 70.)

The MLA Style. If you cite a *general idea* of an entire work, you need mention only the author's name in your text (the body of your paper): Siegel surveys the role of reality television in American culture. You may add Siegel's first name; you *must* add it if you cite two Siegels in your paper.

If you quote, paraphrase, or summarize a *specific fact* or *idea* from a source, cite in your text the author's name and the page from which the material came:

- Direct quotation: According to one recent study, "Reality television is a gospel of relaxation" (Siegel 171). [171 = page. If your paper cites two authors named Siegel, add the first initial.]
- Paraphrase (see 507F, page 68, for definition): Siegel asserts that reality television provides a means of escape for its viewers (171).
- Paraphrase integrating direct quotation: Siegel asserts that reality television is a response to "the oppressive idealizations of celebrity" (171).

Your reader can find full information about the source by turning to your works cited list:

Siegel, Lee. "Reality in America." *Convergences.* Ed. Robert Atwan. Boston, MA: Bedford/St Martin's, 2005. 167–175. [*Convergences* = anthology]

> *Note:* If your works cited list contains more than one entry by the same author(s), give the title before the page number in your citation: (Siegel, "Reality in America" 171). (For a long title, give a shortened version.) For electronic sources that have no paging, give the paragraph number, if any: (Siegel, par. 14). Otherwise, give just the author's name: (Siegel).

The APA Style. If you cite a *general idea* of an entire work, mention the author(s) and year of publication in your text: Siegel (2005) surveys the role of reality television in American culture.

OR

Another study surveys the role of reality television in American culture. (Siegel, 2005).

---

*APA-based material in sections 508–510 Copyright © 2001, 2007, 2010 by the American Psychological Association. Adapted with permission.

If you quote, paraphrase, or summarize a *specific fact* or *idea* from a source, cite in your text the author's last name, the year of publication, and the page from which the material came: `Siegel (2005) asserts that reality television is a response to "the oppressive idealizations of celebrity" (p. 171).`

OR

`According to one recent study, "Reality television is a gospel of relaxation" (Siegel, 2005, p. 171).`

Your reader can find full information about the source by turning to your references list.

Note: If your references list contains two or more entries by the same author(s) with the same publication year, list these entries alphabetically by title (under the author's name) in your references list, and in your citations assign each entry a letter in its reference-list order: `(Siegel, 2005a).`

508B. Avoiding Plagiarism. Plagiarism is taking another **ESL** person's words or ideas without acknowledging that person's authorship. Done intentionally, it is stealing. Even if unintentional, it is a serious violation of research ethics that normally leads to an automatic failing grade or worse. Your reader *must* be able to distinguish between your ideas or words and those of your sources.

Whole papers. You plagiarize when you submit a whole paper that someone else wrote (perhaps from the Internet). Nor should you submit a paper that you wrote for another course (unless your instructor permits).

Paragraphs. You plagiarize also when you lift a whole block of sentences from a source (even in your own paraphrase) and just place a citation at the end. Why is this plagiarism? In the following student paragraph, who is the source of sentences 1 and 2?

`In American culture, reality television is a source of relaxation and a way of resisting the idealization of celebrities. Reality television also celebrates loss, humiliation, rejection, and failure. These are quality experiences in the realm of reality television, and they are a source of comfort for viewers who have undergone similar experiences (Siegel 171-172).`

Actually, the whole paragraph is paraphrased from Siegel, but the student seems to be claiming sentences 1 and 2 as

her own (thus leaving herself open to a charge of plagiarizing them) because she does not state where the material from Siegel *begins*.

Avoid such an accusation by placing a clear acknowledgment of your source at the beginning of the passage—such as `Siegel points out that in American culture. . . .`

Sentences and phrases. You plagiarize whenever you fail to cite a source clearly; that is, when you

*Use a source's **words*** (even with slight changes) as if they were your own, without citing the source.

Original passage (from *Reality in America*, by Lee Siegel): *The "reality" in reality television is a caricature of the idea of reality.*

Student plagiarism—no source cited: `Reality, in the context of reality shows, represents an exaggerated, distorted portrait of the concept of reality.`

*Use a source's **idea**,* even in your own paraphrase, without citing that source. Student plagiarism of Siegel:

`Reality is altered to fit the concept of reality television.`

Fail to enclose the source's exact words in quotation marks, even if you cite your source. Student plagiarism of Siegel—no quotation marks around entire passage: `The "reality" in reality television is a caricature of the idea of reality (Siegel 171).` Even if you take only one distinctive expression, such as "the 'reality' in reality television," without quoting, you have plagiarized.

For legitimate ways to use the Siegel material in your paper, see 508A, page 69. See also 507F, page 68, on paraphrasing.

One aid to avoiding plagiarism: When you take notes, first read and comprehend what the source is saying (or a section of it). Then look away from the source and jot down the source's ideas in your own words. Finally, check what you wrote against the source for accuracy.

509. The Works Cited/References List. Normally, every source you cite in your text must also appear in your works cited/references list, and vice versa. Follow the models in the chart (starting on the next page), noting details such as punctuation and capitalization. Section 510B, page 76, gives sample pages and details of **alphabetizing** entries. Type all works cited/references list entries with a **hanging indent** (first line at left margin, remaining lines indented five spaces or one tab stroke; most keyboarding programs have a "hanging indent" command).

	509A. MLA Style	509B. APA Style

General Principles

Author(s)	Give name(s) exactly as on title page, but reversed (last name first); if two or three authors, reverse only first author's name.	Give only last name and initials of all authors; reverse all names. Use &, not *and*.
Date	Place date with publication data, after title. Abbreviate month.	Place date just after author name(s), in parentheses. Do not abbreviate month.
Title	Use standard capitalization; use quotation marks around short works. *Italicize* full-length works and periodicals. Omit *A, An,* or *The* beginning periodical titles.	Use no capitals in titles and subtitles except for first word and proper nouns. (But do capitalize periodical titles.) Use no quotation marks; *italicize* full-length works and periodicals. Include *A, An,* or *The* beginning periodical titles.
Medium of Publication	At the end of each entry, state its form of publication: `Print, Web, Television, Film, CD, Performance, Address. . . .`	Cite the medium only for certain nonprint sources. See sample entries 17–21.

Sample Entries

	509A. MLA Style	509B. APA Style
Heading →	`Works Cited`	`References`

BOOKS

1. Basic form	`Zapruder, Matthew.` *`Come On All You Ghosts.`* `Port Townsend, WA: Copper Canyon, 2010. Print.` [Copper Canyon = Publisher.]	`Zapruder, M. (2010).` *`Come on all you ghosts.`* `Port Townsend, WA: Copper Canyon Press.`
2. New edition	`Modern Language Association of America.` *`MLA Handbook for Writers of Research Papers.`* `7th ed. New York: MLA, 2009. Print.`	`American Psychological Association. (2010).` *`Publication manual of the American Psychological Association`* `(6th ed.). Washington, DC: Author.` [If author and publisher are the same, just write Author for the publisher.]
3. More than one author (List authors in same order as on title page.)	`Ward, Geoffrey C., and Ken Burns.` *`The War: An Intimate History, 1941–1945.`* `New York: Knopf, 2007. Print.` [For three authors, see item 13. For more than three authors, mention the first author only (followed by a comma) and then say `et al.` (Latin for "and others").]	`Ward, G. C., & Burns, K. (2007).` *`The war: An intimate history, 1941–1945.`* `New York NY: Knopf.` [Give names of all authors up to seven; see item 13. Beyond seven authors, add `et al.`]
4. Editor	`Wintz, Cary D., ed.` *`Harlem Speaks: A Living History of the Harlem Renaissance.`* `Naperville, IL: Sourcebooks, 2007. Print.`	`Wintz, C. D. (Ed.). (2007).` *`Harlem speaks: A living history of the Harlem Renaissance.`* `Naperville, IL: Sourcebooks.`

	509A. MLA Style	**509B. APA Style**
5. Author and editor (Ed.) or translator (Trans.)	Hughes, Langston. *The Collected Poems of Langston Hughes*. Ed. Arnold Rampersad and David Roessell. New York: Knopf, 1994. Print.	Hughes, L. (1994). *The collected poems of Langston Hughes* (A. Rampersad & D. Roessell, Eds.). New York: Knopf.
6. One of several volumes of a book	Burlingame, Michael. *Abraham Lincoln: A life*. Vol. 1. Baltimore: Johns Hopkins UP, 2008. Print.	Burlingame, M. (2008). *Abraham Lincoln: A life: Vol. 1*. Baltimore, MD: The Johns Hopkins University Press.
7. Essay, article, poem, or story in a collection.	West, M. Genevieve. "Zora Neale Hurston." *Harlem Speaks: A Living History of the Harlem Renaissance*. Ed. Cary D. Wintz. Naperville, IL: Sourcebooks, 2007. 115–128. Print. [115–128 = pages on which article is found.]	West, M. G. (2007). Zora Neale Hurston. In C. D. Wintz (Ed.), *Harlem speaks: A living history of the Harlem Renaissance* (pp. 115-128). Naperville, IL: Sourcebooks.
8. Bulletin or government publication	United States. Internal Revenue Service. *Your Federal Income Tax: Tax Guide 2012 for Individuals*. Washington: GPO, 2012. Print. [GPO = Government Printing Office.]	Internal Revenue Service. (2008). *Your federal income tax: Tax guide 2012 for individuals* (IRS publication No. 2012-17). Washington, DC: U.S. Government Printing Office.
9. ENCYCLOPEDIA ARTICLE	Barnd, Natchee Blu. "Shakur, Tupac (1971-1996)." *American Countercultures: An Encyclopedia of Nonconformists, Alternative Lifestyles, and Radical Ideas in U.S. History*. Vol. 3. 2009. Print. [If you used the Web, substitute online title of encyclopedia (no volume), give publisher and year. Medium = Web. Add access date.]	Barnd, N. B. (2009). Shakur, Tupac (1971-1996). In *American countercultures: An encyclopedia of nonconformists, alternative lifestyles, and radical ideas in U.S. history* (Vol. 3, pp. 656-657). Armonk, NY: Sharpe Reference. [If no author given, begin with article title and date. For an online encyclopedia, instead of vol., page, city, and publisher, put Retrieved date from URL.]

PERIODICAL ARTICLES

10. Magazine article (signed)	Abouzeid, Rania. "Cracks in the Armor." *Time* June 11, 2011: 40–41. Print. [40–41 = pages of article.]	Abouzeid, R. (2011, June 11). Cracks in the armor. *Time, 177*(26), 40-41. [177(26) = volume and issue; 40–41 = pages of article.]
11. Magazine or newsletter article (unsigned)	"Depression after Heart Attack: Common, yet Treatable." *Mayo Clinic Health Letter* Feb. 2008: 4–5. Print. [For alphabetizing, see 510B, page 76.]	Depression after heart attack: Common, yet treatable. (2008, February). *Mayo Clinic Health Letter, 26*, 4-5. [For alphabetizing, see 510B, page 76.]
12. Journal article (new paging each issue)	Schwab, Klaus. "Global Corporate Citizenship." *Foreign Affairs* 87.1 (2008): 107–118. Print. [87.1 = vol. 87, issue no. 1.]	Schwab, K. (2008). Global corporate citizenship. *Foreign Affairs, 87*(1), 107-118. [87(1) = vol. 87, issue no. 1.]
13. Journal article (consecutive paging throughout volume)	Same form as item 12. (Give issue number as well as volume number, List authors as follows: Holmboe, Eric S., Rebecca Lipner, and Ann Greiner.)	Holmboe, E. S., Lipner, R., & Greiner, A. (2008). Assessing quality of care: Knowledge matters. *The Journal of the American Medical Association, 299*, 338-340. [299 = vol. 299; 338–340 = pages. Omit issue.]
14. Newspaper article (signed)	McFadden, Robert D. "Strong American Voice in Diplomacy and Crisis." *New York Times* 13 Dec. 2010: 1A+. Print. [1A = section A, page 1; + = "continued on nonconsecutive pages."]	McFadden, R. D. (2010, December 13). Strong American voice in diplomacy and crisis. *The New York Times*, pp. 1A, 33A.

	509A. MLA Style	509B. APA Style
15. Newspaper article or editorial (unsigned)	"Supreme Court to Address California's Prison Woes." Editorial. *San Francisco Chronicle* 1 Dec. 2010: A15. Print.	Supreme Court to address California's prison woes [Editorial]. (2010, December 1). *The San Francisco Chronicle*, p. A15.
16. Review	Sterritt, Brooks. Rev. of *Scorch Atlas*, by Blake Butler. *Redivider*. Spring 2010: 110. Print. [If review has its own title, see the first item in the works cited/references list in 210B, page 76.]	Sterritt, B. (2010, Spring). Review of the book *Scorch atlas*. *Redivider*, 7, 110. [If review has its own title, see the first item in the references list in 210B, page 76.]

NONPRINT MEDIA SOURCES

	509A. MLA Style	509B. APA Style
17. TV or radio show or podcast: single episode or segment of a program or series	"Join or Die." *John Adams*. By David McCullough. Adapt. Kirk Ellis and Michelle Ashford. Perf. Paul Giamatti and Laura Linney. Dir. Tom Hooper. Home Box Office, 16 Mar. 2008. Television. [If your focus is on a performer, writer, etc., you may begin the listing with that name. If not all names are provided, give what you can.]	McCollough, D. (Writer), Ellis, K., & Ashford, M. (Adapters), & Hooper, T. (Director). (2008). Join or die [Television series episode]. In D. Coatsworth & S. Shareshian (Producers), *John Adams*. New York, NY: Home Box Office. [Do not give narrators or performers. If a podcast, after title put Podcast retrieved from, then channel letters and colon (if TV), then URL.]
18. Song recording or podcast	Bell, Joshua, and Frankie Moreno. "Eleanor Rigby." By John Lennon and Paul McCartney. *Joshua Bell at Home with Friends*. Sony, 2009. CD. [You may begin with performer, composer, etc., depending on your focus. Add recording date, if it precedes publication date, before CD title.]	Lennon, J., & McCartney, P. (2009). Eleanor Rigby. [Recorded by Joshua Bell and Frankie Moreno.] On *Joshua Bell at home with friends* [CD]. New York, NY: Sony. [Add recording date, if it precedes publication date, in parentheses at end of entry.]
19. Motion picture, videotape, or DVD	*No Country for Old Men*. Dir. Ethan Coen and Joel Coen. Perf. Tommy Lee Jones, Javier Bardem, and Josh Brolin. Miramax Films-Paramount, 2007. DVD. [If your text focuses on a star, director, or producer, you may begin the entry with that person's name. For the video or DVD, omit the film distributor and Film, but after the original release date give the video or DVD distributor and date; end with DVD or videocassette. E.g....Brolin. 2007. Paramount, 2008. DVD.]	Coen, E., & Coen, J. (Producers & Directors). (2007). *No country for old men* [Motion picture]. United States: Miramax Films-Paramount. [Or use Videotape or DVD in place of Motion picture.]

ONLINE SOURCES

Note on online sources: Use Web for the medium. Omit the URL unless the reader may not otherwise find the site. (Put such a URL in angle brackets at the end of the entry: <http://www.gutenberg.org/dirEtext/963>.

Line-break a URL only after a slash. Use no hyphens.) If no date or publisher is given, use n. d. or N. p. For an online encyclopedia entry, see item 9.

Note on Web addresses (URLs): Use no angle brackets. Use no period at end. Use no hyphen when breaking a URL at the end of a line. Break a URL only before punctuation, but keep http:// together.

Follow title with Retrieved (give date), from (give enough of the URL for easy retrieval of the item). (If date you accessed item is same as publication date, omit retrieval date.) If source text will not be altered (such as a book or journal article), omit date after Retrieved. In most cases, the home page URL is enough.

509A. MLA Style	509B. APA Style
	DOI: Some journal articles now give a Digital Object Identifier (DOI) on first page. Put this DOI (type `doi:`) in place of URL. You may have to click a box such as Article to get the DOI.
20. Electronic mail	Foster, Arlene R. "Using Semicolons Between Clauses." Message to the author. 10 Apr. 2010. E-mail.	[Put email communications from individuals as personal communications in the text: A. R. Foster (personal communication, April 10, 2010). Do not include email in the references list.]
21. Online posting (newsgroup, blog, online discussion group, electronic mailing list, etc.)	Sarafatti, Jack. "Cahill's Claims of Absolute Motion and Nanotechnology Tests." Online posting. 15 Mar. 2008. [If group has a title, give it here, underlined.] Web. 21 Mar. 2010.	Sarafatti, J. (2008, March 15). Cahill's claims of absolute motion and nanotechnology tests. Online posting. Retrieved from http://groups .google.com/group/sciphilosophy .tech
22. Personal or professional website or page	Petaschnick, JoAnn. "Understanding Sepsis." *MCW Healthlink*. 26 Jan. 2005. Medical College of Wisconsin. Web. 9 Dec. 2010. [Quoted part = Web page title; italicized part = site title. First date = publication date or latest update; second = date of access. If site has no title, give a description, such as Home page—not underlined.]	Petaschnick, J. (2005, January 26). Understanding sepsis. *MCW Healthlink*. Retrieved December 9, 2010, from http://healthlink.mcw .edu/article/1031002466.html [Date in parentheses = publication date or latest update. If necessary, give the kind of site in brackets (e.g., [Fact sheet] or [Press release]) after title, before period. Retrieval date is given because site can be updated.]
23. Article (or abstract) from a professional journal (electronic or originally in print)	Taylor, Christopher. "North America as Contact Zone: Native American Literary Nationalism and the Cross-Cultural Dilemma." *Studies in American Indian Literatures* 22.3 (2010): 26–44. *Project MUSE*. Web. 4 Sept. 2010.	Taylor, C. (2010, Fall). North America as contact zone: Native American literary nationalism and the cross-cultural dilemma. *Studies in American Indian Literatures, 22*(3), 26–44. Retrieved from http://muse .jhu.edu/journals/studies_in _american_indian_literatures
24. Newspaper article	Broder, John M. "Official Says U.S. Won't End Drilling Ban in Eastern Gulf." *New York Times* 1 Dec. 2010. Web. 2 Dec. 2010.	Broder, J. M. (2010, December 1). Official says U.S. won't end drilling ban in eastern gulf. *The New York Times*. Retrieved from http://www.nytimes.com
25. Online book	Dickens, Charles. *Little Dorrit*. London, 1857. Project Gutenberg Etext. Web. 12 Nov. 2010.	Dickens, C. (1997). *Little Dorrit*. Retrieved from www.gutenberg.org /etext/993 (Original work published 1857) [1997 = year of Internet publication. If URL leads only to how to obtain book, use `Available from`, not `Retrieved from`.]

See additional samples in 510B, page 76.

For resources to help you master this section's topics, log in to www.mywritinglab.com and select Research Process from the list of subtopics.

510. Setting Up the Pages. Sample pages of text and bibliography are shown below. Double-space everything. Unless your instructor directs otherwise, make your top, bottom, and side **margins** one inch wide, except for the page number at the top right, which is a half inch from the top (usually preceded by your last name in MLA style or the first few words from the title in APA).

510A. Text Pages

MLA Style. Unless told otherwise, put your heading (your name, instructor's name, class, and date) at the top left of page 1. Center the title below that; do not repeat the title on subsequent pages:

> Rodriguez 1
>
> Amelia Rodriguez
> Professor Fast
> Native Lives
> 29 November 2012
>   The Restoration of a Personal and Cultural
>   Tlingit Sense of Place
>   Language provides the tools necessary for en-
> tire cultures to declare themselves into existence.
> This declaration, oral or written, is the key to each
> culture's developing a sense of place. A sense of
> place emerges from the connection between physical
> places and the language that their inhabitants use to
> describe them. Having a sense of place is especially
> important for the Tlingit, an indigenous people of
> the Pacific Northwest coast, because they rely on the
> natural environment for their livelihood, making their
> connection with the land a key aspect of their cul-
> ture, tradition, and survival. This paper will examine
> selected writings to illustrate that development.
>   In her book *Life Woven with Song*, Nora Marks
> Dauenhauer develops a Tlingit sense of place, as well
> as a personal one, and can even be said to transform
> that personal sense. She illustrates that this sense
> might be rooted in the concept and process of writing
> as well as in the culture's more traditional prac-
> tices of subsistence (34).

APA Style. Unless told otherwise, start with a separate title page containing the following information, centered, above the middle of the page:

> Title of paper
>
> Your name, with middle initial
>
> Course title
>
> Instructor's name
>
> Date

Count this page as page 1. In the upper right corner of this and every page, put the first few key words of your title and the page number. At the beginning of the first page of text, repeat the title:

> Tlingit Sense of Place 2
>   The Restoration of a Personal and Cultural
>   Tlingit Sense of Place
>   Language provides the tools necessary for entire
> cultures to declare themselves into existence. This
> declaration, oral or written, is the key to develop-
> ing a sense of place. A sense of place emerges from
> the connection between physical places and the lan-
> guage that inhabitants of those places use to de-
> scribe them. Having a sense of place is especially
> important for the Tlingit, an indigenous people of
> the Pacific Northwest coast, because they rely on
> the natural environment for their livelihood, making
> their connection with the land a key aspect of cul-
> ture, tradition, and survival. This paper will exam-
> ine selected writings to illustrate that development.
>   Dauenhauer, in *Life Woven with Song* (2000),
> develops a Tlingit sense of place, as well as a
> personal sense of place, within the boundaries of
> a written text. It is even quite possible that
> Dauenhauer transforms her sense of place in the
> book, and illustrates that her sense of place might
> be rooted in the concept and process of writing, as
> well as in more traditional practices of subsistence
> (p.34).

510B. Works Cited/References List Pages.

510B. Works Cited/References List Pages. Alphabetize all entries in one list, according to the last name of the author. (If a work has more than one author, alphabetize by the author named first on the title page.) If a work gives no author, alphabetize by the first word of the title (other than *a, an, the*).

MLA Style. After the first line of an entry, **indent** all lines five spaces or one tab stroke (a hanging indent). If two or more entries are by the same author, give the author's name for the first of these entries only; for the other(s), in place of the author's name type three hyphens and a period (---.). Alphabetize these entries by the first word of the title (other than *a, an, the*). See sample listings below.

APA Style. As with MLA, indent each line after the first line five spaces or one tab stroke (a hanging indent). But if two or more entries are by the same author, list them by date, the earliest first; repeat the author's name each time. See sample listings below.

MLA Style

Rodriguez 11

Works Cited

Cardiff, Gladys. "Nora Marks Dauenhauer's *Life Woven with Song*." Rev. of *Life Woven with Song*, by Nora Marks Dauenhauer. *Studies in American Indian Literatures* 16.2 (2004): 65–73. *Project MUSE*. Web. 9 Dec. 2008.

Dauenhauer, Nora Marks. *Life Woven with Song*. Tucson: U of Arizona P, 2000. Print.

---, and Richard Dauenhauer, eds. and trans. "Introduction." *Haa Shuka, Our Ancestors: Tlingit Oral Narratives*. 1987. Vol. 1 of *Classics of Tlingit Oral Literature*. Seattle: U of Washington P, 1987. 3–59. Print.

Parker, Robert Dale. "Another Indian Looking Back: A Review Essay on Recent American Indian Poetry." *Studies in American Indian Literatures* 22.2 (2010): 75–85. Print.

Russell, Caskey. "Tools of Self Definition: Nora Marks Dauenhauer's 'How to Make Good Baked Salmon.'" *Studies in American Indian Literatures* 16.3 (2004): 29–46. *Project MUSE*. Web. 7 Feb. 2010.

Taylor, Christopher. "North America as Contact Zone: Native American Literary Nationalism and the Cross-Cultural Dilemma." *Studies in American Indian Literatures* 22.3 (2010): 26–44. *Project MUSE*. Web. 4 Sept. 2010.

Thornton, Thomas F. *Being and Place Among the Tlingit*. Seattle: U of Washington P, 2008. Print.

Womack, Craig S. "A Single Decade: Book-Length Native Literary Criticism between 1986 and 1997." *Reasoning Together: The Native Critics' Collective*. Norman: U of Oklahoma P, 2008. 3–105. Print.

APA Style

Tlingit Sense of Place 11

References

Cardiff, G. (2004, Spring). Nora Marks Dauenhauer's *Life woven with song* [Review of the book *Life woven with song*]. *Studies in American Indian Literatures, 16*(2), 65–73.

Dauenhauer, N. M. (2000). *Life woven with song*. Tucson: The University of Arizona Press.

Dauenhauer, N. M., & Dauenhauer, R. (1987). *Haa shuka, our ancestors: Tlingit oral narratives*. Seattle: University of Washington Press.

Parker, R. D. (2010, Summer). Another Indian looking back: A review essay on recent American Indian poetry. *Studies in American Indian Literatures, 22*(2), 75–85.

Russell, C. (2004). Tools of self definition: Nora Marks Dauenhauer's "How to make good baked salmon." *Studies in American Indian Literatures, 16*(3), 29–46. Retrieved from http://muse.jhu.edu/journals/studies_in_american_indian_literatures

Taylor, C. (2010, Fall). North America as contact zone: Native American literary nationalism and the cross-cultural dilemma. *Studies in American Indian Literatures, 22*(3), 26–44. Retrieved from http://muse.jhu.edu/journals/studies_in_american_indian_literatures

Thornton, T. F. (2008). *Being and place among the Tlingit*. Seattle: University of Washington Press.

Womack, C. S. (2008). A single decade: Book-length Native literary criticism between 1986 and 1997. In *Reasoning together: The native critics' collective* (pp. 3–105). Norman, OK: University of Oklahoma Press.